# RADICAL Christianity
## Peace and Justice in the New Testament

*Daniel M. Keeran*

Counsellor Publishing
Vancouver, British Columbia
Canada

Copyright © 2006, by Counsellor Publishing.

All rights reserved. No part of this book may be used or reproduced in any manner whatsoever without specific written permission from Counsellor Publishing except in the case of brief quotations in reviews for inclusion in a magazine, newspaper, or broadcast.

---

**Keeran, Daniel M., 1947-**
  **Radical Christianity : peace and justice in the New Testament / by Daniel M. Keeran.**

**Includes bibliographical references and index.**
**ISBN 0-9734546-5-2**

  1. Peace--Biblical teaching.  2. Social justice--Biblical teaching.  3. Bible. N.T.--Criticism, interpretation, etc.  I. Title.

BS2545.P5K44 2006    241'.6242    C2005-905692-4

---

Printed in the United States. For publication and ordering write to:

Counsellor Publishing,
76024, 1358 West Georgia Street
Vancouver, BC, Canada V6E 4S2
or email **counsellor@uniserve.com**

*This book is dedicated to my loving
wife, daughter, and son
and to all who have shared
the call of discipleship.*

# Table of Contents

| | |
|---|---|
| Introduction | 7 |
| **Part I: Radical Justice Economics** | **13** |
| Chapter 1 - The Kingdom of God as a Radical Social Movement | 15 |
| Chapter 2 - Decisions For The Poor | 35 |
| Chapter 3 - Of Interest and Profit | 51 |
| Chapter 4 - The Rich Young Ruler Revisited | 69 |
| **Part II: Radical Peace Politics** | **81** |
| Chapter 5 - The Ethic of Non-Violence: The Christian Dynamic for Social and Political Order | 83 |
| Chapter 6 – Peacemaking In Action: How To Manage Conflict | 115 |
| Chapter 7 – The Peaceable Kingdom: A Bible Concordance for Pacifists | 133 |
| **Part III: Radical Applications** | **183** |
| Biblical References | 191 |
| Bibliography: Primary and Secondary Sources | 195 |
| Index | 199 |
| About the Author | 205 |

# Introduction

The title of this volume is redundant because message of Jesus Christ that calls together a people, is itself a radical call to follow. The teaching of Jesus is radical because it is not of this world. It is a call to take up one's cross, to deny oneself, and to forsake everything one possesses (Lk.9:23; 14:33).

The nature of this divine message is that it rejects and stands in contrast to many of the central and commonly accepted values and beliefs of culture and society. The term sacrificial could accurately be used to describe this way of life, as radically different than the pleasure-seeking theme of the world today as when the Word first appeared.

Although the instructions of Jesus for his disciples may be thought harsh and discomforting, he says, "My yoke is easy and my burden is light," perhaps because of the simplicity of life and the peace borne of an eternal hope (Matt. 11:30).

Within a movement always seeking a return to biblical roots, the Christian community today must do more than replicate the external patterns and words of the apostolic period. A sincere response realizes a need to restore also the life and deeds that proceed from the love of God. In all aspects of God's will for his people in both form and function and in both minor areas of obedience and weightier matters of justice, Jesus says, "These you ought to have done, and not left the other undone" (Matt. 23:23).

From the close of the apostolic age the witness of the early Christian writings referenced in this volume, is clear regarding the role of rich and poor in the kingdom and the non-violent nature of Christian conduct. After the legalization of Christianity and decline of paganism in the fourth century, the church began to swell with rich and powerful members of Roman society. The church reacted to the compromise of its values, in the development of monasticism that allowed those truly devoted to God to maintain a poverty lifestyle while accommodating others in their lifestyle of comfort.

Contemporary with this and in common usage today, a doctrine of justifiable warfare was defined by Augustine to support Christians as combatants in the military. History has shown that any war can be easily and subjectively spun as a war of defense against evils seen in any society.

In spite of many dark pages of history, the implications of Jesus' original message have not been lost. In his book *The Tradition and*

*History of Churches of Christ in Central Europe,* Dr. Hans Grimm who was himself descended from twelfth century Christians in the Alsatian region of France, documents the faith and life of those who "resolved to stand by the Saviour's way of non-violence" and held that "those possessing goods should live as though they possessed nothing."

The present volume is divided into three parts: the first addressing the radical principles of personal finance, the second pertaining to the non-violent way of the cross, and the third looking briefly at specific ideas created to live out the meaning of the crucified life of love for others. The second part includes a chapter on practical approaches for peacemaking in relationships as well as a concordance of words in scripture related to pacifism intended to assist the reader in further study of the biblical text in all its depth and impact "piercing to the division of soul and spirit, of joints and marrow" in the life of the disciple (Heb. 4:12).

## A Word of Caution

In the application of radical Christianity, there are various dangers and pitfalls. There may be a tendency to interpret the teachings as requiring works in order to earn or deserve salvation. This view can be corrected by remembering the words of Jesus who said, "So you also, when you have done all that is commanded you, say, we are unworthy servants; we have only done what was our duty" (Luke 17:10).

In application of the principles in this book, the disciple may err in other ways. A few examples are: lending to those not truly in need, viewing all business ventures as wrong, seeking out persecution when it can be avoided to achieve the ends of the gospel, and giving away all of one's income and assets leaving one completely dependent upon others. Other common errors are to use the peace and justice teachings as a personal attack on individuals or, conversely, to apply them to political systems rather than accepting them as an individual life style decision. Jesus did not come to establish a political or economic system, but to transform the person.

The sincere effort to live sacrificially calls for divine wisdom to be obtained through many prayers of faith (James 1:5,6). The best intentions are difficult to pursue and fulfill when one attempts alone and without support. Much prayer, devotion, study and the encouragement of likeminded friends are needed. There are examples among saints of old who have ventured forth equipped with an undying faith and commitment to follow Jesus unto death regardless of the persecution and ridicule they suffer along the way of the cross.

# *Part I*

# *Radical Justice Economics*

# 1

*The Kingdom of God as a Radical Social Movement*

## Not Of The World

Reality as defined by Jesus was in conflict with the reality defined by ancient society. Yet it was precisely because the early church lived according to the divine definition that the kingdom of God was a radical element in the world. Christians were not products of society then and must not be so today, for society is a human product. Its institutions, acceptable forms, and attitudes are largely constructed by man, not God. That is why the kingdom of God is a radical movement faithfully resisting assimilation that otherwise occurs through the process of socialization and acculturation whereby society tends to mold and determine, however subtly at times, the values of groups and individuals within its sphere of influence.

Secular culture brings about a certain conformity of values through various pressures and structures such as public education, the media, entertainment industry, civil law, patriotic sentiment, technology and the politico-economic system. To be a radical, one who casts doubt upon and challenges socially constructed values, means to suffer loneliness and abuse. Although this is their calling (II Tim. 3:12), many Christians have found it much easier, with little or no cost emotionally and psychologically, to conform to the world than to shape their lives according to the divine construction of reality.

## The Beginnings

That the kingdom of God would be characterized by a radical social orientation is suggested as early as the conception of Jesus by the virgin Mary who said in her magnification of God, "He has filled the hungry with good things but has sent the rich away empty" (Lk. 1:53). Whether or not this was a prophetic utterance, it summarizes Jesus' ministry as far as His teachings and personal instructions regarding the rich and poor are concerned.

In fact, it would seem that the central purpose of Jesus' ministry was to bring the gospel to the poor, for Jesus himself announced this as the purpose of His being "anointed" prophet, high priest, and king (Lk. 4:18). Later when John the Baptist sent messengers to inquire whether Jesus was the promised Messiah, the proof for John was to be that the sick were being healed and "the good news is preached to the poor" (Lk. 7:22).

John the Baptist himself realized this emphasis of the coming kingdom, for as he prepared the people of Israel for the new age, he said, "The man who has two coats should share with him who has none, and the one who has food should do the same" (Lk. 3:10,11). This was the "fruit worthy of repentance" (Lk. 3:8) for those who were to accept the rulership of the Messiah. In order to be a recipient of the kingdom, a beneficiary of the gospel and blessed of God, one was called upon to distribute his wealth among those who lacked.

## *The Distribution of Personal Wealth*

The ministry of Jesus was also for the purpose of preparing a people for the kingdom, and he required the same fruit as His forerunner. To the rich young ruler he said, "You still lack one thing. Sell everything you have and give to the poor, and you will have treasure in heaven. Then come, follow me" (Lk. 18:22).

When the wealthy tax collector Zaccheus had made his commitment, Jesus declared, "Today salvation has come to this house" (Lk. 19:8,9). It can be inferred that Zaccheus had given all after he had restored four-fold to those from whom he had taken by fraud, in addition to half his possessions to be given outright to the poor. Zaccheus had an infamous reputation for exacting more tax than was due, so that by the time he had kept his promise he was indeed among the ranks of the poor for whom the kingdom was prepared. The radical response of Zaccheus indicates that Jesus' proclamation of the gospel included a call for radical commitment in terms of the distribution of one's own wealth.

The disciples closest to Jesus were given this same call, the same "fruit worthy of repentance" required by John the Baptist. Jesus instructed his little flock, "Sell your possessions and give to the poor. Provide purses for yourselves that will not wear out, a treasure in heaven that will not be exhausted, where no thief comes near and no moth destroys" (Lk. 12:33). The rich young ruler, on the other hand, rejected this kingdom call and was "sent away empty" (Lk. 1:53).

## A Kingdom For The Poor

The gospel and the kingdom were for the poor, and in order for the rich to enter, they were called upon to divest themselves of their wealth by distributing it to the needy. That the kingdom belongs to the poor is specifically mentioned by Jesus in the sermon on the plain where it is written, "Blessed are you who are poor, for yours is the kingdom of God" (Lk. 6:20).

Later, James reminded his readers of this fact when he wrote, "Listen, my dear brothers: has not God chosen those who are poor in the eyes of the world to be rich in faith and to inherit the kingdom he promised those who love him?" (Jas. 2:5). This was James' argument in correcting those in the church who showed favoritism to rich visitors in the assembly. James says that it is the poor, not the rich, who are the very heirs of the kingdom. The rich may not receive it unless they bear the required fruit and thereby join the ranks of the poor as Zaccheus, the rich young ruler, and other disciples of Jesus and John the Baptist were enjoined to do.

That both the kingdom and its ministry are for the poor is expressed by Jesus in an interesting set of instructions concerning the giving of a feast. "When you give a luncheon or dinner, do not invite your friends, your brothers or relatives, or your rich neighbors; if you do, they may invite you back and so you will be repaid. But when you give a banquet, invite the poor, the crippled, the lame, the blind, and you will be blessed. Although they cannot repay you, you will be repaid at the resurrection of the righteous" (Lk. 14:12-14). Jesus continues in the same passage by referring to the kingdom as a feast and explains that it is for the same kinds of people that his followers are to invite to their fellowship suppers.

The rich and those preoccupied with worldly concerns are not welcome to the feast of the kingdom (Lk. 14:15-24). Indeed only the poor can be disciples of Christ, for the cost of being a disciple requires that one sell all and distribute unto the poor: "Any of you who does not give up everything he has cannot be my disciple" (Lk. 14:33).

## *The Rich Must Become Poor*

Unless the rich assume the same life style as the poor, in terms of things possessed, they have no place at the feast. While the poor are "filled with good things" in being promised the kingdom and treasure in heaven, the rich are "sent empty away" in being refused a place at the banquet table. In the midst of a hungry, thirsty, crying world, the rich have chosen to be filled. "You have lived on earth in luxury and self-indulgence. You have fattened yourselves in the day of slaughter" (Jas. 5:5).

The rich cannot receive the kingdom while they comfort themselves with luxury and abundance in a world of suffering and want. The rich are truly "sent away empty" as Jesus says, "But woe to you who are rich, for you have already received your comfort" (Lk. 6:24). In the account of the rich man and Lazarus, the former is condemned not for trusting in his wealth but merely for keeping and enjoying it. This point is summarized by Clement of Alexandria (190 A.D.) who wrote, "It is wrong for one to live in luxury while others are in want" (Instructor II.xiii.20.3 and 6).

Having sent the rich young ruler "empty away" after setting before him the demands of the kingdom, Jesus explains how utterly impossible it is for a rich man to enter the kingdom. "Again I tell you, it is easier for a camel to go through the eye of a needle than for a rich man to enter the kingdom of God" (Mat. 19:24). The ensuing conversation seems, perhaps somewhat indirectly, to reveal how it is possible for the rich to be saved. "I tell you the truth, no one who has left home or wife or brothers or parents or children for the sake of the kingdom of God will fail to receive many times as much in this age and, in the age to come, eternal life" (Lk. 18:29,30). In order to find his life one must lose it (Mat. 10:39). In order for the rich man to be saved and find true wealth, he must lose his material wealth to those who lack.

So far we have seen that the message of the kingdom from the beginning of its proclamation demands a life style of poverty or subsistence living, not as an end in itself but as the result of selfless giving to those who lack. John instructed his people to keep just enough for personal warmth and nourishment (Lk. 3:10.11), and Jesus required His followers to sell all and distribute to the poor. This is consistent with the fact that the gospel and the kingdom are for the poor according to Jesus' own statements (Lk. 4:18;6:20).

## *Abundant Giving Defined*

The idea of a subsistence life style is also to be inferred from Jesus' definition of abundant giving. It is said that a certain poor widow, who gave out of poverty, had given more than all those who cast into the treasury out of their abundance (Lk. 21:1-4). Only if the rich had given also to the point of subsistence could it have been said that they had given as much as the widow. Therefore, to "sow abundantly" (II Cor. 9:6) or to be liberal or "rich in good works" (I Tim. 6:18) means to give all, thus implying a poverty life style.

## *Food and Clothing*

Paul also indicates that for themselves Christians are to be concerned only with maintaining those possessions that provide simple nourishment and warmth, life-supportive elements. "But if we have food and clothing, we will be content with that" (I Tim. 6:8). The writer of Hebrews also encourages his readers, "Keep your lives free from the love of money and be content with what you have, because God has said, Never will I leave you; never will I forsake you" (Heb. 13:5). This emphasis stands in opposition to attitudes ancient and modern that encourage and justify the pursuit and accumulation of wealth. James speaks of "needs" in terms of food and clothing, nourishment and warmth (Jas. 2:15,16). This same pairing is found also in the preaching of John the Baptist (Lk. 3:10,11) and the teaching of Jesus (Mat. 6:25; 25:35-45). The poor are understood to be those who live according to their needs, as defined above, rather than according to their desires or above their needs.

## The Imitation of Christ

Yet a certain material life style is not in itself the aim of the Christian but is the actual result of abundant giving and of perfect love for the lost and suffering. Paul suggests that a poverty life style is in imitation of God's own grace. As he urged the Corinthians to give for the alleviation of want among the Jerusalem saints, Paul wrote, "For you know the grace of our Lord Jesus Christ, that though he was rich, yet for your sakes he became poor, so that you through his poverty might become rich" (II Cor. 8:9) In addition to this example of Christ, Paul held up the example of the Macedonians who had given "beyond their means" (vs.3).

The new Jerusalem church, having received God's gracious gift, could do no less than respond in imitation of that grace. "There were no needy persons among them. For from time to time those who owned lands or houses sold them, brought the money from the sales and put it at the apostles' feet, and it was distributed to anyone as he had need" (Acts 4:34,35). Jesus in the parable of the merciless servant teaches that he who is shown God's grace is expected to respond by extending grace to others (Mat. 18:23-33). The New Testament church could do no less than follow the example of Jesus in becoming poor that others might be made rich.

The grace of Jesus therefore provides the rationale and the motivation for a subsistence life style. The teaching that prepared a people for the coming kingdom, continued to be applied after the kingdom had come and God's grace had been manifested in the death of Jesus. The kingdom life style then received added impetus, for the precedent of giving all had been set by Jesus himself, the king and the author of our salvation. The apostle John explains that the love of God does not dwell in the Christian whose material life style does not reflect the mercy of our Lord in giving himself, his all upon the cross (I Jn. 3:16, 17).

## *The Purpose of Abundance*

Paul writes that one's abundance is a gift of God's grace that is given not to keep but to distribute in turn "unto every good work" (II Cor. 9:8). God supplies and multiplies one's seed in order that it might be sown (II Cor. 9:10). He makes you "rich in every way" for the purpose of liberal giving, not sumptuous living (II Cor. 9:11). To live a life of luxury in the midst of human misery is to embezzle God's grace. The faithful use of God's abundance results in one's having no more than enough "as it is written: he who gathered much did not have too much, and he who gathered little did not have too little" (II Cor. 8:15). The abundance of one is to be the supply for another's needs (II Cor. 8:14), and any other use of one's abundance is in spite of the grace God has shown to him.

The kingdom of Israel was promised to and established among the poor of Israel, and the kingdom can be successful today only as a poor people's movement. When middle and upper classes fill the kingdom without divesting themselves of their class distinctions, in terms of their possessions, they defeat the ministry of the church by a life style that mocks the grace of God.

## *A Reversal Of Social Order*

According to the scriptural evidence, it would seem the kingdom of God on earth is intended to bring about a reversal of the social order.[1] Those who are of the lowest class, according to socially constructed socio-economic values, are given an exalted place in the kingdom while those esteemed in the world in terms of social status, are made low. In the kingdom the humble are exalted, the exalted are made low; the poor are blessed, the rich are cursed; the highest office is that of servant (Mk. 9:35; Mat. 23:12). The last are first and the first are last.

The middle and upper classes of worldly society can rejoice in the kingdom only when they fulfill their role as servants in the distribution of their wealth, for in being made low they too acquire an exalted place with the poor. "The brother in humble circumstances ought to take pride in his high position. But the one who is rich should take pride in his low position, because he will pass away like a wild flower" (Jas. 1:9,10).

## *The Biblical Work Ethic*

The very purpose of laboring is itself in order to permit the labourer to exercise his servant role in providing for those who are weak and in need. The former thief is enjoined to work in order to be able to give to those in need (Eph. 4:28). If this is the purpose of his labour, we who are not former thieves can do no less. Paul also left us his own example in advocating that just as "these hands served my own needs and those who were with me... that by this kind of hard work you must help the weak" (Acts 20:35). The biblical work ethic then does not give one the right to enjoy everything he works for, but lays upon him the obligation to serve and to distribute the fruits of his labor among those who lack.

The New Testament church understood its servant role as the called-out kingdom of God. Its life style reflected the reception of God's grace, and its ministry as the saved poor to the lost poor was realized. The church remained faithful to this mission for a time, and then like many radical movements, it came to terms with the world and ceased to be an effective force toward the continued realization of the kingdom of God.

## Second Century Radical Christianity

Into the second century Christians received the radical calling of the Messianic community with Jesus' definition of reality with the child-like naiveté that Jesus requires of those who would enter the kingdom (Mk. 10:13-16). Clement of Rome (96 A.D.) said he knew of many who had sold themselves into slavery in order to use the money to feed the hungry, and some had sold themselves into bondage to purchase freedom for others (Clement, *Epistle to the Corinthians*, 55:2).

The Shepherd of Hermas (135 A.D.), alluding perhaps to Jesus' way of salvation for the rich man (Mat. 19:29), said to his readers, "Therefore instead of fields, purchase afflicted souls, as each is able. And visit widows and orphans and do not neglect them. Spend your wealth and all your possessions on such 'fields and houses' which you receive from God. For the master made you rich for this purpose that you might perform these ministries for him" (*Similitudes*, I:8f). The Shepherd of Hermas understood accurately the servant role of the rich, the purpose of riches, and the cost of discipleship that have been discussed.

Another second-century document known as the *Preaching of Peter* contains this admonition: "Understand then you rich, that you are in duty bound to do service, having received more than you yourselves need. Learn that to others is lacking that wherein you superabound. Be ashamed of holding fast what belongs to others. Imitate God's equity and none shall be poor."[2] Possessions in excess of that which one needs are said to belong not to the holder but to others who lack.

Irenaeus (180 A.D.) did not believe Christians were obligated to tithe but that Jesus made a more stringent demand. "And instead of the tithes which the law commanded, the Lord said to divide everything we have with the poor... and to be liberal givers and sharers not only with the good but also to be liberal givers toward those who take away our possessions" (*Against Heresies*, IV, xiv, 3). Irenaeus understood Jesus' demand of the rich young ruler to apply to all disciples.

Clement of Alexandria (190 A.D.) was outspoken in his understanding of kingdom realities. "And it is not right for one to live in luxury while others live in want. How much more glorious is it to do good to many than to live sumptuously! How much wiser to spend money on human beings than on jewels and gold!" (*Instructor* II, xiii, 20.3 and 6). Many other references from the writings of the early post-apostolic church show that the social radicalism of the kingdom was still being adhered to well into the second century.[3]

## *Jesus Calls The Church Today*

The church today must become poor, and it must address itself to the poor. It must live among the poor in the ghettos and inner cities. The church must "spend its wealth and all its possessions on such fields and houses." For the gospel is for the poor and the kingdom belongs to the oppressed, the sick, the suffering, the lost, the humble, the hungry, the abased, those of low social standing. Instead, the church has made its company with the rich in the suburbs. It has said to the rich, "Sit thou here in a good place," while the poor are left far away in the inner city and have not even the privilege of sitting at our feet. The charge of James applies to the church today: "you have insulted the poor" (Jas. 2:3,6).

Today the visible church is composed of a social class that was never invited to the feast and that was not intended to receive the kingdom. The rightful heirs of the kingdom and true objects of the church's ministry are shut out by distance and "good taste." The odours and filth of the poor are not complimentary of the fine halls that give worldly status to the church. The church has shut out the poor and is itself shut out of the feast of the kingdom. The church lacks mercy and this poverty condemns it. The church thanks God for her riches and does not know that she is "wretched, pitiful, poor, blind and naked" (Rev. 3:17).

In order for Christians to realize the kingdom of God within themselves, they must "produce fruit in keeping with repentance." Those who have two coats and more food than they need must give to those who lack. If the church rejects this call, the Christ will send it "away empty." In turn, the demand Jesus made of the rich young ruler and of Zaccheus is the demand the church must make, and like those two, the rich must either repent and distribute their wealth to the needy or be refused entrance and fellowship.

Those who reject the kingdom call have trusted in their riches, for they have coveted wealth and luxury above the souls and lives of men. The accumulation of unnecessary material possessions is done to the neglect of the needy who are "always with us" (Jn. 12:8). The alternative to trusting in riches is to distribute them to the poor. In so doing, one lays up for himself true riches (Lk. 18:22; 12:33; 19:8,9). Paul in writing to Timothy also relates abundant giving and sharing to "laying up treasure for themselves as a firm foundation for the coming age, so that they may take hold of the life that is truly life" (I Tim. 6:19).

Jesus instructs his followers not to lay up treasure on earth, but to lay up for themselves these treasures in heaven (Mat. 6:19,20). Those who decide to keep His abundant material trusts for their own selfish use are the objects of eternal woe (Lk. 16: 19-25) while those who give them for the alleviation of human suffering receive God's blessing and salvation (Lk. 19:8,9).

Jesus' teaching to "sell all and distribute to the poor" is considered by many to be an ideal, unattainable or unworkable in real life socially constructed. The choice for us is whether to follow the divine construction of reality viewed by society to be radical, unrealistic, and impractical or to be socially constructed individuals whose life styles are mere recordings and playbacks of socially acceptable forms and attitudes.

## NOTES

[1] See Richard Batey's discussion of the "theology of reversal" in Jesus and the Poor (New York: Harper and Row, Publishers, 1972), pp. 18-22

[2] Arthur O. Lovejoy, The Journal of the History of Ideas (Oct. 1942), pp.461-462.

[3] See the chapter entitled, "Early Christian Acts of Mercy," in Everett Ferguson's Early Christian Speak (Austin: Sweet Publishing, 1971), pp. 207-218.

# 2

*Decisions For The Poor*

In recent decades, a number of benevolent organizations and non-religious efforts, have made extensive appeals for contributions from the public. Undoubtedly, we will see more presentations of this kind as world population increases and as the gap widens between rich and poor nations. Every Christian must now ask this question, "What does God expect of *me* in view of the millions who are starving right now?"

*Good News For The Poor*

To answer this question, we will begin with a Messianic passage found in Isaiah 11, verse 4: "With righteousness he will judge the needy, with justice he will give decisions for the poor of the earth." One of the primary ministries of the Messiah was to bless the poor. The place of rich and poor in relation to the Messianic kingdom is introduced by Mary's magnification of God and by the first preaching of John the Baptist and of the Christ himself.

Mary affirms that God has "scattered those who are proud in their inmost thoughts" and that he has brought down the powerful and "sent the rich away empty." Moreover, she declares, God has "lifted up the humble' and has "filled the hungry with good things" (Luke 1:51-54).

When John the Baptist appears, he refers to Isaiah 40:3-5 as his program of ministry. John understands that his purpose is to prepare the way of the Lord by a type of landscaping that brings down mountains and hills while the valleys are exalted or filled in. This is reminiscent of Mary's statement, for when the multitude inquire about the proper fruit of repentance, mountains and hills are lowered and valleys are exalted as John instructs the people to distribute their abundance to the poor. Even specific groups among the crowd are divested of their lucrative incomes as John exhorts soldiers and tax collectors to cease extortion, to collect only the tax due, and to be content with meager wages (Luke 3:4-14). The powerful and rich are brought down and sent empty away while the poor and humble are filled with good things and lifted up, even as Mary had declared concerning the justice of God.

When Jesus appears, he refers to Isaiah 61:1,2 as his program of ministry. Jesus understands that he is "anointed to bring good news to the poor" (Luke 4:18ff). Since the term "Messiah" actually means "anointed one," Jesus is announcing that good news for the poor is at the very heart of his teaching and preaching ministry. Jesus corroborates the statement of Isaiah 11:4 that he will make "decisions for the poor of the earth." In fact, the proof for the imprisoned John that Jesus was indeed the expected Messiah was that Jesus was fulfilling the prophecy of Isaiah 61: 1,2, for he was blessing the afflicted and preaching the Gospel to the poor (Luke 7:21, 22).

The Gospel message of Jesus to the poor themselves is this: "Blessed are you who are poor, for yours is the kingdom of God" (Luke 6:20). These are not the spiritually poor but the literally poor, for in the same address Jesus pronounces a woe upon the literally rich (v. 24). That the poor filled the kingdom is verified by James 2:5: "Listen, my dear brothers: has not God chosen those who are poor in the eyes to world to be rich in faith and to inherit the kingdom he promised to those who love him?" It is not surprising that James again echoes Jesus in pronouncing the strongest condemnation on the rich: "Come now, you rich, weep and wail because of the misery that is coming upon you" (James 5:1).

## *A Costly Response Demanded*

The message of the New Testament to the rich demands a costly response, for the rich enter the kingdom and benefit from the Gospel only as servants of the poor. This is clear from the very beginning of the preaching of the Gospel of the kingdom, for those who have must distribute to those who have not, in order to receive John's baptism (Luke 3:10-11).

To all his disciples Jesus says, "Lay not up treasure on earth...but lay up for yourselves treasure in heaven" (Matt. 6:19f). To the little flock Jesus explains how treasure is laid up in heaven: "Sell what you have and give to the poor" (Luke 12:33). The rich young ruler was given the same instruction: "Sell your possessions and give to the poor, and you will have treasure in heaven" (Matt. 19:21). To the Pharisees, Jesus declared, "Give what you have to the poor, and all will be clean for you" (Luke 11:41). The mandate of Jesus' earthly ministry is clear: in order to be assured of eternal life, heavenly treasure, spiritual cleanness, the rich must distribute their abundance to the poor.

Zaccheus, the rich tax collector, received salvation - treasure in heaven - by responding to this new ethic of the Messianic kingdom. He made a commitment to distribute his wealth to the poor and to those whom he had oppressed. Surely, by the time he had kept his promise to restore four-fold to those he had wronged, Zaccheus would find himself among those to whom the kingdom belongs (Luke 19:8,9). Because of the radical response of Zaccheus, we can infer that he had heard Jesus preaching a radical commitment in terms of distributing one's wealth to the poor.

Indeed, those who store up treasure for themselves on earth rather than distributing to the poor are like the rich fool of whom Jesus speaks. To sacrifice one's affluence for the poor is to be "rich toward God" (Luke 12:21; Matt. 25:40). The rich do not give abundantly and acceptably until they give as the widow who gave all she had (Mark 12:41f). This teaching from the account of the widow's mite should be regarded as providing the definition of liberality and "sowing abundantly," as Paul later enjoins (II Cor.9:6). The widow, however, was not resigned to death by starvation, for her support came from the temple treasury, but her degree of giving reinforces what Jesus has said about the obligation of the rich to give out of their need level, which means all of their abundance and then some.

In the parable of the unjust steward Jesus teaches powerfully that to withhold God's trust of worldly wealth from those in need is embezzlement, and the consequence is to be denied true riches. "I tell you," he said, "use worldly wealth to gain friends for yourselves, so that when it is gone, you will be welcomed into eternal dwellings" (Luke 16:8-12).

Jesus then immediately gives warning to the wise in the illustration of the rich man and Lazarus. The fate of the rich man who failed to come to terms with worldly wealth illustrated Jesus' pronouncement of woe upon the rich, for they have already received their comfort in this life (Luke 16:19-25; 6:24). The rich man died and was refused entrance into eternal dwellings. His worldly wealth was gone, and he had not been trustworthy.

It is in the context of what is said in the parable of the unjust steward, illustrated again by the rich man and Lazarus, that we must understand Jesus' teaching about serving two masters. Serving God is using "worldly wealth to gain friends," thus being "trustworthy with someone else's [God's] property"(Luke 16:9,12). Serving mammon or wealth is withholding God's trust from the poor, preferring rather to live in luxury and comfort in a world of suffering and want (Luke 16: 19-25).

The injunction to distribute one's abundance makes it impossible to keep God's property for self and maintain trust in God. This is the meaning of Jesus' statement that "you cannot serve God and wealth" (Luke 16:13). He who chooses to keep God's possessions, has despised God and his will for the affluent: "What is highly valued among men is detestable in God's sight" (Luke 16:15). Giving, not out of one's wealth, but out of one's need, is the teaching of the Kingdom from the words of John the Baptist to the widow who gave a fraction of a penny.

A universal principle of discipleship is stated in Luke 14:33: "Any of you who does not give up everything he has cannot be my disciple." Jesus is calling upon prospective followers to forsake, relinquish, or renounce the possession of earthly goods. He is not here speaking of family relationships as in verse 26, because the Greek phrase for "everything he has" refers to literal material possessions or earthly goods. "The expression always (fourteen times) denotes earthly goods in the New Testament" (G. Kittel, ed., *Theological Dictionary of the New Testament*, Vol. 8, p. 33). The same principle is stated in other words when Jesus commends laying up heavenly treasure instead of, not in addition to, earthly treasure (Matt. 6:19).

## *Generosity Of Early Christians*

Not only does this emphasis pervade the Gospel accounts, but it is also found throughout the New Testament. The immediate response of the first Christians was to determine that all things would be held as common property. This meant that they sold their possessions and gave to the poor. The result was that no one among them was in need (Acts 2:44, 45; 4:32, 34, 35). Ananias and Sapphira felt compelled to do what was being done by others: selling and giving. Laying the money at the apostles' feet was not compulsory, but was simply one method of distribution. Yet there was perhaps a degree of status attached to the act, at least in the minds of this couple, who were prompted to go so far as to lie about having given all (Acts 4:32- 5:11).

Eventually during a long famine, the saints in Jerusalem had spent their resources. Paul then tried to encourage the same kind of giving from the Corinthians as had occurred earlier in Jerusalem, suggesting that the sincerity of one's love in giving is to be measured or defined by the example of the Macedonians, who gave out of "their extreme poverty" (II Cor. 8:2), and by the example of Christ himself, who "though he was rich, yet for your sakes he became poor..." (v.9).

Paul does not want to command or compel the Corinthians to give in this way, because he wants them to be willing and cheerful in their giving (II Cor. 8:12; 9:7). Yet the expectation is clear in terms of the degree of giving Paul wants from them, for he continues by urging, "At the present time your plenty will supply what they need... as it is written, he that gathered much did not have too much, and he that gathered little did not have too little" (II Cor. 8:14,15). Further, Paul emphasizes the importance of sowing generously, defined by the preceding examples of Macedonia and of Christ, which reflect Jesus' definition of abundant giving in the example of the poor widow who gave more than the rich because she gave what she needed to live on.

## *The Source And Purpose Of Wealth*

Paul identifies God as the source of one's abundance, and the purpose of God's gift is two-fold: (1) to provide for the needs of the one who receives from God, and (2) to allow the one who receives to provide for the needs of others (Acts 20:34-35; Eph. 4:28). The rich have received from God, not to increase their enjoyment of luxury and comfort, but to increase their distribution unto "every good work" and so they "can be generous on every occasion." It is through the generosity of the rich that God "has scattered abroad his gifts to the poor" (II Cor. 9:8-11). When the rich neglect to do this, they have embezzled God's gifts and fail in their servant role.

In his first letter to Timothy, Paul suggests that generosity and good deeds enable one to lay up treasure in heaven – reminiscent of Jesus' instruction to the little flock, the rich young ruler, and all disciples (Matt. 6:19ff). Notice that rather than being rich in the possession of wealth, the affluent are to be rich in the giving of those possessions (1 Tim. 6:17-19). Certainly, Paul could not have meant less than Jesus meant in his definition of generosity.

John makes a similar point. Those who live in luxury and abundance in spite of the suffering of the poor do not have God's love within them (I John 3:16,17). While John emphasizes this responsibility to the poor brother, the New Testament clearly extends the demonstration of love to all men (Gal. 6:10;

II Cor. 9:13; I Thess. 3:12). The love and grace of Christ find reality in the believer's life when he sacrifices his possessions as Christ did (I John 3:16; II Cor. 8:9).

Giving as the Macedonians, Christ, and the poor widow gave, will reduce us to a simple life style, with basic necessities and minimal possessions (I Tim. 6:8). Luxury and self-indulgence are among the sins of the rich (James 5:5). Christians are specifically forbidden to wear expensive clothes and jewelry (I Pet. 3:3; I Tim. 2:9-10). According to Jesus, those who have already received their comfort in this life will find no comfort in the next life (Luke 6:24; 16:19-25). But those who are caring and generous can know the blessedness of giving (Acts 20:35) and the assurance of the Lord's promise never to abandon us (Heb. 13:5).

In the book of Revelation, the church of Laodicea claims to be rich and in need of nothing because of her accumulated wealth. But Jesus assesses her situation differently: "You do not realize that you are wretched, pitiful, poor, blind and naked. I counsel you to buy from me gold refined in the fire, so you can become rich" (Rev. 3:17-18). One can convert earthly riches into "gold refined in the fire" by distributing one's wealth to the poor.

## The Abominations Of Babylon

The abominations of Babylon the Great are a final reminder of the thesis of this study. The rich and powerful are clearly and intimately associated with the sinful city. "The kings of the earth committed adultery with her, and the merchants of the earth grew rich from her excessive luxuries" (Rev. 18:3). God's people must not share in her sins (v. 4). She will receive "as much torture and grief as the glory and luxury she gave herself" (v. 7). In her day of judgment, Babylon the Great will mourn with all those who became rich through her wealth (v. 7,9,19). Here we see fulfilled the truth of Jesus' words: "Woe to you who are rich, for you have already received your comfort" (Luke 6:24).

Moreover, Mary's words at the beginning of the New Testament are strangely fulfilled in this closing vision of Babylon, for the rich and powerful are brought down and sent empty away. In Babylon is seen the fate of all who live in luxury at the expense or neglect of the world's poor. On the other hand, God's faithful poor and those who distribute their wealth according to God's purpose can look forward to the comfort and luxury of the New Jerusalem, the heavenly treasure for those who have invested wisely.

## *Attitudes Of The Early Church*

Isaiah promised Messianic decisions for the poor, and we have seen their fulfillment in the words of Mary, John the Baptist, the Messiah himself, Paul, James, the apostle John, and in the deeds of the Jerusalem and Macedonian churches.

The early church writers from the close of the New Testament through the time of Constantine soundly support the biblical teaching concerning the place of rich and poor in the kingdom of God. Clement of Rome (96 A.D.) observed that many Christians had sold themselves into slavery in order to buy food for others. Aristides (120 A.D.) pointed out that early Christians fasted in order to send their food to the poor (see *Apology* 15). The Shepherd of Hermas (136 A.D.) affirmed that God gave abundance to the rich so that they could spend their wealth and "all their possessions" to relieve others (see *Similitudes*, I:8f). In the *Epistle to Diognetus*, 10:4,5 (140 A.D.) the affluent are instructed to distribute the things received from God, to help those in need. In the *Preaching of Peter* (180 A.D.) it is said that the abundance of the rich belongs to the poor. Clement of Alexandria (190 A.D.) said it is not right for one to live in luxury while others are in want (see *Instructor* II.xiii.20:6).

In *Against Heresies*, IV.xiv.3, Irenaeus (180 A.D.) expressed the following: "And instead of the tithes which the Law commanded, the Lord said to divide everything we have with the poor." (See the chapter entitled, "Early Christian Acts of Mercy," in Everett Ferguson's *Early Christians Speak*, Austin: Sweet, 1971).

## Conclusion

The clear perspective of the kingdom with regard to wealth has remained obscure to many. Perhaps this is partly because preachers whose salaries are paid by the rich, have sought to please and accommodate the rich. If so, the advice given to the church of Laodicea is appropriate for us. We must obtain gold from our Lord that we may become truly rich. We must flee from the destruction of Babylon and partake in her sins no longer. May God help us as we seek always to have less of this world that we may possess more of the kingdom of God. We will realize more of his Kingdom when we have lived by his "decisions for the poor of the earth."

# 3

# *Of Interest and Profit*

One of the continuing struggles of those who wish to be God's people is to rediscover and to practice the values and norms of the Kingdom of God, often in direct conflict with the prevailing notions of the majority culture. In some areas of thought that have especially wide-ranging implications, many Christians have adopted the secular assumptions without questioning their morality in the light of Scripture. Pragmatism is the spouse of the secular mind-set and is an important criterion for approved behavior within the framework of culture and religion in North America today.

The secular mind-set assumes conduct to be proper simply because it works for contemporary society. This study calls into question one major assumption of secular society: that the profit motive is morally acceptable. An examination of the Old Testament literature will be followed by an exposition of New Testament teaching and a summary of the historical development of thought from the time of the early church to the Stone-Campbell movement.

## Old Testament Teaching

The Old Testament discusses the profit motive in terms of interest and increase. The earliest teaching seemed to prohibit only the taking of interest and increase from a poor fellow Israelite, and initially only taking interest was ruled out.

> *If you lend money to one of my people among you who is needy, do not be like a moneylender; charge him no interest.*
> Exodus 22:25

In the book of Leviticus, however, we see the prohibition expanded somewhat to include profit: "You must not lend him money at interest or sell him food at a profit" (Lev. 25:37). Still later in the Pentateuch, the instruction is expanded further to include a ban on interest on anything loaned to any brother Israelite, not just to the poor.

> *Do not charge your brother interest, whether on money or food or anything else that may earn interest. You may charge a foreigner interest, but not a brother Israelite.*
> Deuteronomy 23:19,20

During the period of the united kingdom one of the characteristics of the ideal citizen of Zion was that he did not lend his money at interest (Psalm 15:5). The poverty or affluence of the borrower had no bearing on the morality of lending at interest, but certainly the consequences for the poor are greater than for the rich when interest is charged. In whatever era, interest and profit contribute to inflation, thus grinding the face of the poor by increasing the cost of food and shelter. However, in Solomon's observation that "he who augments his wealth by interest and increase gathers it for another who will be kind to the poor" (Prov. 28:8), there seems to be a progression or broadening of the law regarding interest and profit.

Perhaps the strongest pronouncement against interest and increase, is a statement of the prophet Ezekiel, especially enlightening because at that time Israel was in exile among a foreign people. Much of its trading and business was with foreigners from whom the Mosaic law permitted Israel to take interest. Excavations at Nippur of ancient Babylon have uncovered a business house whose inscriptions reveal many Jewish names, thus indicating how thoroughly the Jews were adapting and being assimilated into the business practices of the country (Nicol, T., "Captivity," in *The International Standard Bible Encyclopedia*, 1929 ed., Vol. I, p.574).

Perhaps responding to the Jews' adoption of Babylonian business ethics, Ezekiel advocated that those who loaned for interest and who took increase or profit should be put to death (Ezek. 18:8, 13, 17). Finally, during the period of the return from exile, Nehemiah tried to eliminate even small interest, only one percent, on loans among the people.

> *Moreover I and my brethren and my servants are lending them money and grain. Let us leave off this interest. Return to them this very day their fields, their vineyards, their olive orchards, and their houses, and the hundredth of money, grain, wine, and oil which you have been exacting of them.*
>
> Nehemiah 5:10-11

To summarize the Old Testament teaching: a gradual expansion of the law against interest and increase seems to have occurred from the time of the Exodus to the period of the Exile. At first, the law prohibited taking interest only from the poor Israelite and only on food and money. Later, the law prohibited taking interest from any Israelite on anything loaned. Still later, during the Exile, we find a blanket condemnation of those who take any interest and increase, even though God's people were doing much of their business with foreigners. Also, it is important to recognize that no distinction between interest and usury is made in any of the biblical literature. Rather, interest in any amount is considered excessive in the above contexts. The notion of acceptable and unacceptable levels of interest, the latter referred to as usury in modern usage, did not develop until the late Middle Ages.

## New Testament Teaching

The link between the Old and New Testaments on the subjects of lending, interest, and profit is to be found in the teachings of Jesus in the Gospel accounts and in the writings of Paul. In the Sermon on the Mount and the Sermon on the Plain, Jesus summarizes the magnified ethics of the Kingdom of God. He reverses, for example, the teaching on seeking recompense for wrongs and says that his disciples should practice non-violence. Adultery is committed in thought, not simply in the physical act, and harm lies in destructive anger, not just in murder. With this kind of insight into the reality of progressive revelation, one may approach the expanded implications of Jesus' teaching on lending and giving.

In the teaching account recorded in Luke 6, Jesus states the requirement of the Mosaic law: that we ought to lend not only to friends but also to enemies. But he goes quite beyond that when he suggests that every loan is to be regarded as a gift. Whereas in the Old Testament Israel was taught to lend without expecting interest in return, Jesus teaches we are to "lend without expecting to get *anything* back."

> *Give to everyone who asks you, and if anyone takes what belongs to you, do not demand it back...if you lend to those from whom you expect repayment, what credit is that to you? Even sinners lend to "sinners," expecting to be repaid in full. But love your enemies, do good to them, and lend to them without expecting to get anything back.*
>
> Luke 6:30-35

Demanding interest goes far beyond merely expecting to get some return. Therefore, this teaching not only prohibits interest but also eliminates even the expectation of getting the principle back or a return loan (see G Kittel, ed., *Theological Dictionary of the New Testament*, 1964 ed., vol. 2, p.534).

This meaning of the Lukan passage is reinforced by Jesus' use of the Greek word *daneizo* for "lend" in verse 35. According to W.E. Vine (*Expository Dictionary of New Testament Words*, 1966 ed., s.v. "Lend, Loan"), *daneizo* refers to money "loaned on security or return." The article on "Lend, Loan" in the *International Standard Bible Encyclopedia* (Ibid., Charles B. Williams, Vol.III, p.1865) points out that *daneizo* refers to money loaned "usually in a commercial sense." If Jesus had wanted to use a word for lending as a friendly act or for immediate personal needs, small amounts or items which one would not expect back, he would have used the word *kichremi* as in Luke 11:5, where a person asks a friend for bread to feed his guests.

We see then that the Mosaic law against interest is greatly amplified by Jesus' concept that the lender should regard every loan as a gift, thus precluding receiving interest as a moral option. The lending to which Jesus refers involves major loans, those which one would usually expect to receive again and with interest. Thus, *daneizo* is to be regarded with the same attitude as *kichremi*. Moreover, this kind of lending is to be extended to all men, regardless of their relationship to God.

Another point of contact between the Old and New Testaments is found in Ezekiel and in several passages in Paul's letters. In Ezekiel 22:12 and elsewhere the Septuagint, with which the New Testament writers were certainly familiar, uses the word group including *pleonexia* and *pleonektes* to translate into Greek the Hebrew term for "unjust gain." Here the idea of interest and increase have the clear connotation of *unjust* gain.

> *In you men accept bribes to shed blood; you take interest and increase and make unjust gain from your neighbors by extortion. And you*

*have forgotten me, declares the Sovereign Lord.*
Ezekiel 22:12

Paul also speaks with extreme disfavor toward those who engage in *pleonexia*, translated "greed" or "covetousness" in many English versions. He tells the Ephesians that "among you there must not be even a hint of...any kind of...*pleonexia*" (Eph. 5:3), and that those who practice such will not enter the Kingdom of God. (See also I Cor. 5:10, 11, 6:10; Col. 3:5-7.) Paul need not mention interest and increase specifically, because "a hint of...any kind of" includes all specific acts associated with *pleonexia*.

The literal root meaning of *pleonexia* is "over reaching." When New Testament writers used this Greek word, they often meant "having too much," as well as *receiving* or *wanting* too much; this would suggest "over reaching" through interest and profit, unjust gain. This connotation must have persisted at least until the time of Origen in the third century, for he used *pleonektes* to refer to one who takes interest, the usurer (TDNT, ibid., vol. 6, pp.269-270).

## Early Church Teaching

With this strong background of teaching against every kind of greed as well as the idea that every loan be regarded by the lender as a gift, it is no surprise that the early church from the second century to the Renaissance vigorously opposed the taking of interest and profit. Quoting Ezekiel 18:4-9, where it is attested that the man who does not oppress anyone, who returns what he took in pledge for a loan, who does not lend at usury or take excessive interest is righteous and will live, Clement of Alexandria affirms that by following the prohibition of interest, the new convert will find eternal life.

In opposing the views of Marcion, Tertullian attempting to show the harmony of the Old and New Testaments, compared Luke 6:34-35 to Ezekiel 18:8, stating that "the purpose of the law laid down by Ezekiel was to prepare for the Gospel, to lead men to the perfect discipline of Christ." Tertullian's reasoning was that interest was prohibited in the Old Testament in preparation for the expanded teaching of Christ concerning loans (Robert P. Maloney, "The Teaching of the Fathers on Usury," *Vigilliae Christianae* 27 [1973]: 243-244). This same strong opposition to taking interest is seen throughout the early writings and has been well documented through the time of Augustine in the fifth century. The teaching against interest recognized no exceptions and was wrong even if the borrower was rich (Ibid., p. 264).

In the thirteenth century, the canonists of the Roman Catholic Church adapted their church's teaching to the growing secularism with regard to interest and profit. Until then, the church insisted that the price for goods should be just, defined as "the cost of the material plus the value of the labor expended on it." Anything over this was considered profit and was unjust gain. But by the time of the high Middle Ages and early Renaissance, the rise of wealthy merchant companies, banking houses, and guilds led to the justification of raising prices to cover the risk of loss through piracy and shipwreck, for example. In a similar manner, the opposition to lending on interest gave way to "elaborate and sometimes devious exceptions developed by the canonists to allow interest under certain conditions... Like the history of the just price, the history of usury illustrates the gradual triumph of secular over religious values." (R.S. Hoyt, Europe in the Middle Ages [New York: Harcourt, Brace and World, 1957], pp. 435-436).

Today, few professing Christians would question the conclusion of the Roman Church lawyers. Even the Reformation leaders, who protested the corruption of the Roman Church, firmly resisted the attempts by certain "extremists" of the time to restore the prohibition of interest. Luther and others apparently feared such a teaching would discredit their efforts in the eyes of secular powers. (Benjamin Nelson, *The Idea of Usury*, Chicago: University of Chicago Press 1969, p.29).

## Restoration Teaching

In the Stone-Campbell movement Barton W. Stone and Jacob Creath, Jr. expressed their views in the pages of the *Christian Messenger*. Referring to the prohibition of lending for interest, Stone wrote, "This was one of the laws of God given to his people of old. Never was a practice more explicitly condemned. It may be asked, is this law binding on Christians? If it is, why was it not incorporated among the laws of the New Institution? I answer, it is binding, and it is incorporated among the laws of Christ, greatly magnified or enlarged (Luke 6:34)." Stone states further that "the door of heaven will be shut and barred" against those who seek to rise above "the standard of humble Christians" (June 1843, pp. 48-51).

Alexander Campbell, on the other hand, expressed the majority opinion in his *Millennial Harbinger* and employed a number of assumptions in his pragmatic approach to the issue. The major assumption was that if money is loaned to a rich man who intends to use it for trade, commerce, or speculation, then interest in morally acceptable (June 1843, p. 258). A basic unquestioned assumption is that Christians may lend to a rich man who is not in need. Another assumption is that a Christian may himself engage in profit-making and speculation. Campbell does not refer to the significance of *daneizo* and *pleonexia*, but he at least admits that a poor man should not be charged interest. This admission would place Campbell outside current practice; yet as the richest man in West Virginia, Campbell certainly had a stake in justifying commercial lending and interest.

Campbell and many of his heirs sought New Testament approval for taking interest by citing the parable of the talents in Matthew 25 and Luke 19. Campbell asserts that the practice of receiving "interest for money loaned is altogether right, else the Lord could not have represented himself (as the austere master) as having received it" (Ibid.,p.257). The problem with Campbell's reasoning is two-fold. First, Jesus is no more teaching that trading for profit and receiving interest are moral options than he is teaching that one may become an unjust judge "who neither fears God nor cares about man," yet the latter parable represents God himself as that unjust judge (Luke 18:1-8). Nor is Jesus recommending that anyone become a thief, yet this is a metaphor Jesus uses for himself as a "thief in the night."

The second difficulty with Campbell's reasoning is that the master in the parable of the talents is in fact depicted as *one who over reaches*, for he is described as "a hard man, taking out what you did not put in, and reaping what you did not sow." Based upon this description of himself, the master says to his servant, "Why then didn't you put my money on deposit, so that when I came back, I could have collected it with interest?" (Luke 19:20-23). Certainly a major point is that taking interest is in keeping with the character of greed: "taking out what I did not put in" (v. 22).

*Conclusions*

From this study, a number of conclusions can be drawn. A progression or broadening of the prohibition against interest seems to have occurred within the Old Testament period. In the New Testament Jesus precludes taking interest as a moral option when he requires that the lender should regard every loan as a gift. Paul condemns every kind of greed, and from the connotation of the Greek word *pleonexia*, this would seem to include a prohibition of interest and increase.

The early church continued to oppose taking interest and profit as avarice, and this attitude did not change until secular influences triumphed in the decisions of Roman church lawyers in the thirteenth century. The Reformation leaders, seeking to satisfy secular powers, opposed any suggestion to restore the prohibition of interest. In the Restoration Movement, the majority are the heirs of

Alexander Campbell, who accommodated the secular assumptions whereas a minority represented by Barton W. Stone and Jacob Creath, Jr., opposed interest and speculation.

Greed cannot be separated from the profit motive. Profit is by definition unearned, and the teaching of the New Testament is that we must live by our own personal labour rather than the labour of others: "If a man will not work, he shall not eat" (II Thess. 3:10). Paul points out to the Ephesian elders that he had supplied his own needs and the needs of his companions and had worked hard to be able to help the weak (Acts 20:30-35).

The idle rich are no better than the idle poor. The notion that money works or that money can be put to work is parallel to the ancient Greek idea that money can produce offspring (Eager, George B., "Bank, Banking" in ISBE, Vol. I, p.383). Even today, reference is made to the ability of money to "bear" interest. These are examples of the secular rationale for the exploitation of labour and consumer and for the justification of greed. Those who receive interest and profit are living off the labour of consumers and workers, for it is people who work, not money.

The profit motive seeks to minimize the cost of labour in order to maximize profits. James speaks with the zeal of Ezekiel in pronouncing judgment upon the rich who minimize the wages of labor: "Look! The wages you failed to pay the workmen who mowed your fields are crying out against you" (Jas. 5:4).

An alternative to the profit motive or incentive is the service motive whereby one seeks to minimize profit. Whereas service as a motive is the very definition of the character of Christ, profit as a motive is the very definition of greed and is a root of economic upheaval in any society. If we are to be the body of Christ and a light to the world, we must reflect his character and follow his leading rather than the pragmatic norms and values of secular society and culture.

# 4

# *The Rich Young Ruler Revisited*

Occasionally in our reading and teaching of God's word, we tend to soften the difficult demands of Jesus. An example of this has been our handling of the account of the rich young ruler to whom Jesus said, "If you want to be perfect, go, sell your possessions and give to the poor, and you will have treasure in heaven. Then come, follow me" (Matt. 19:21).

These words were as disappointing to that young man as they are to many of us today, and so we have performed some theological engineering to dull the sharp edge of the Spirit's sword. Here is how our popular "prophets" defend us against Jesus' threat to our comfortable way of life. A biblical exposition will follow each defense.

**1) *Jesus spoke these words only to the rich young ruler.***
The instruction to the rich young ruler appears to be a teaching of the new age of the kingdom and a universal condition of discipleship (Lk.14:33). At the beginning of the preaching of the kingdom, John the Baptist had made a similar demand of the multitudes who came to his baptism. He charged them, "He who has two coats, give to him who has none, and he who has food, let him do likewise" (Lk.3:10,11).

In his own ministry, Jesus told his closest disciples to sell their possessions and give to the poor in order to have treasure in heaven (Lk.12:33). He also told the Pharisees to give what they had to the poor, and everything would be clean for them (Lk.11:41).

After listening intently from his perch, Zaccheus responded to radical social teachings when he committed his wealth to the poor and oppressed, and Jesus' reply was, "Today, salvation has come to this house" (Lk.19:8,9). In the sermon on the mount, Jesus instructed all his followers to lay up treasure in heaven rather than on earth (Matt.6:19-21).

In the account of the rich young ruler, in Jesus' statement to his close disciples, in his declaration to Zaccheus, and in Paul's charge to the rich, we learn that laying up heavenly treasure is accomplished by selling our possessions and giving to the poor or becoming rich in good deeds (I Tim.6:17-19). In order for the rich to give liberally or abundantly and thereby lay up a foundation for eternal life, they have the example of the poor widow who gave much or liberally because she gave out of what she needed to live on or from a poverty life style (Mk.12:41-44).

**2) *Jesus said it is hard, not impossible, for the rich man to enter the kingdom of heaven.***
According to the preaching of the kingdom, the door to heaven is too small for

the affluent to enter having enjoyed a life of luxury and comfort. Not to be found in sermons today, Jesus pronounced the woe of judgment upon the rich in the sermon on the plain where he said, "Woe unto you rich, for you have already received your comfort" (Lk.6:24).

This woe is vividly portrayed in the account of the rich man and Lazarus. Both men died and the tables were turned with the rich man in torment and the beggar in comfort (Lk.16:19-25). Jesus used a powerful figure to emphasize how absurd it is to think that the rich can go to heaven, when he said, "It is easier for a camel to go through the eye of a needle than for a rich man to enter the kingdom of God" (Matt.19:23).

***3) The eye of a needle refers to the sheep gate in the wall of Jerusalem. It was hard but not impossible for a camel to pass through that gate.***

The sheep gate was never referred to as the needle's eye until centuries after Jesus' statement. Rather Jesus was using an expression employed by contemporary rabbis to illustrate the impossibility of an act or event ever occurring. It is the idea of the largest known animal passing through the smallest known opening. In North Africa, the rabbis spoke of the impossibility of an elephant passing through the eye of a needle (cf. G.

Kittel, ed., *Theological Dictionary of the New Testament*, Vol.III, p. 593). In Palestine the largest animal was the camel. Hence Jesus' metaphor says in effect that entry into the kingdom of God is completely impossible for the rich.

**4) The rich can be saved in spite of their possession of wealth because Jesus said with God all things are possible.**

When Jesus stated the impossibility of the rich entering heaven, the disciples asked, "Who then can be saved?" The popular notion was that if anyone could be saved it would be the rich upon whom God has showered his favour and blessing. Jesus' teaching about the rich not entering heaven left the disciples thinking no one could be saved.

How then is it possible for God to save the rich? God is able to save the rich if they are willing to do God's will in laying up heavenly treasure by sacrificing their affluence for the poor. The disciples declared they had left everything, and so Jesus promised salvation to them and to anyone (Matt.19:29), as he did to Zaccheus for the same reason.

In his closing remarks in this passage, Jesus said, "But many who are first will be last, and many who are last will be first" (Matt.19:30). Those who are first in this world, the affluent, will be last which means excluded while those who are last in this life, the righteous poor and those who sacrifice their affluence, will be first in the kingdom.

**4) Mark's account of the rich young ruler says that "trust in riches" is what will exclude the rich from heaven. So it is possible to enjoy comfort and luxury, yet still trust in God and be saved.**

Trust in riches is the greatest obstacle for the rich who want to enter the kingdom. This is because trusting in God means doing what God has said and commanded: sell your possessions and give to the poor. Jesus' command to distribute one's affluence makes it impossible to keep one's affluence and still trust in God. This is the meaning of Jesus' statement: "You cannot serve both God and wealth." One will despise one or the other. He who chooses to keep his possessions has despised God and his will for the affluent. That which is highly valued among men is an abomination to God (Lk.16:13-15).

### Taking Jesus' Teaching Seriously

Let us no longer be guilty of filtering Jesus' teaching through our modern-day materialistic thinking. We must admit that we are shaped by the majority culture and society in which we live. This society is worldy because of the "the desire of the physical body, the desire of the eye, and the pride of life" (I John 2:16). Our tendency is to compromise in order to fit in and be acceptable to the world, and in so doing we lose our saltiness and our light becomes dim.

In a world of increasing hunger and poverty, it is time for us to realize that our own eternal salvation depends upon our active recognition of the Saviour's calling to sacrifice our affluence for the poor. Yes, Jesus came to save the lost, but on the other side of the coin that speaks of the promise of eternal life, there is the message of social responsibility.

As servants of Christ, James says our justification requires faith-ful-ness or a working faith. Not that we can earn or deserve salvation by doing good, for after we have done all that is commanded, we must say, "We are unworthy servants; we have only done what was our duty" (Lk.17:10). But can we be saved if we refuse to do our duty? Let James answer: "You see that a man is justified by works and not by faith alone" (James 2:24).

John the Baptist and Jesus stand in the line of Hebrew prophets and have brought their cry for social justice to completion. In fact, Jesus began his ministry with the reading of the Jubilee passage from Isaiah 61:1,2 that says, "The Spirit of the Lord is upon me, for he has anointed me to preach the gospel to the poor" (Lk.4:18). That these are the literal poor is attested by Luke 7:22 where preaching good news to the poor was proof for John the Baptist's disciples that Jesus is the Christ. The good news was of course that the kingdom of God belongs to the poor (Lk.6:20).

Jesus had no faithful disciples who were rich. Two rich men remained secret disciples because they feared the Jews (Jn.12:42,43; Jn.19: 38,39). Rich men in the Old Testament were sometimes approved by God for three reasons: 1) Jews were responsible only for the poor within Israel, 2) God provided for a Jubilee year when property was to be redistributed to the original owners and all debts were cancelled, 3) God enacted detailed legislation providing for the poor and the stranger within Israel (Lev.25: 8ff). In the New Testament, on the other hand, Jesus' teaching seems to call for a continual practice of the Jubilee spirit as people distribute their abundance upon entrance into the kingdom.

Certainly what Jesus and John the Baptist were asking of their disciples was unlike anything we find in the Old Testament in terms of the extent of giving of one's possessions. Yet the roots of this teaching are clearly seen in the law and the prophets. The practice of this new kind of sharing is seen in the example of the Jerusalem and Macedonian churches (Acts 4:32; II Cor.8: 1-4). The Corinthian church is exhorted to follow the example of Macedonia who gave out of "extreme poverty" (II Cor.8: 2) and of Jesus himself who "though he was rich, yet for your sakes he became poor…" (II Cor.8: 9).

Does this mean that Christians and those who would be disciples of Christ must quit their jobs, crawl into a corner, and starve to death? On the contrary, the message of the New Testament is that we must work to provide necessities for the poor, our families, and ourselves (Acts 20:34,35; Eph.4: 28; I Tim.5:8). If we are dead, we cannot help anyone.

Jesus was certainly not telling the rich young ruler to starve to death, but rather to divest himself of his affluence for the sake of the poor. This would mean that henceforth he would live only according to his basic needs as enjoined by Paul: "If we have food and clothing, we will be content with that" (I Tim.6:8). Paul taught disciples of Christ to live the same material lifestyle and accept the same social responsibility that Jesus himself taught.

The simple life, becoming poor for the sake of the poor, is the consistent admonition of the New Testament from the preaching of John the Baptist, the teaching of Jesus, Paul, James, and John. Even Mary praises God because he is on the side of the poor and powerless and against the powerful and rich (Lk.1: 52,53).

All the patterns of sound doctrine are needed, especially what pertains to the weightier matters of justice and mercy. Let us restore these biblical ideals to our teaching, preaching, and practice in the Messianic community. As we fulfill the social message of the good news, Jesus invites us and says as he did to the rich young ruler, "Then come, and follow me" (Matt.19: 21).

# Part II

# Radical Peace Politics

# 5

*The Ethic of Non-Violence:
The Christian Dynamic for
Social and Political Order*

The kingdom of God introduced an ethic designed to deliver the earth into the hands of the meek (Mat. 5:5). Disciples of Jesus were instructed in the practice of non-violence, to turn the other cheek in the face of oppression (Mat. 5:39), and the early church understood this ethic to preclude Christians' participating in the government as judges, plaintiffs, or soldiers.[1] Instead of the use of force to change men and to defend the weak, the early church believed in the power of spiritual weapons such as love, kindness, gentleness and meekness (II Cor. 10:1-5). This ethic has long been lost because of centuries of socialization.

Now Christians openly advocate the use of physical coercive means to change the evils of society. Christians go to war, form a majority to oppress a minority, go to court against their neighbours, and legislate morality to bring the world into line by threat of force. Instead of the power of love, gentle persuasion, and meekness, modern Christians employ government legislation, courts, guns, jails, and fines with which to change the world and to seek justice.

The cost that discipleship demands is higher than many people are willing to afford, for in the patient endurance of oppression, the oppressed follow Jesus in his suffering: "When they hurled their insults at him, he did not retaliate; when he suffered, he made no threats.

Instead, he entrusted himself to him who judges justly"(I Pet. 2:23). Sometimes God's approval in the patient endurance of wrongs, is the only consolation for the oppressed (I Pet. 2:21). Jesus calls people not to comfort and safety, but to suffering and sacrifice, to deny themselves and take up the cross, to lose their lives and find life (Mat. 16:24,25).

## *Peace In Old Testament Prophecy*

In prophecies concerning the Messiah and his kingdom, the themes of peace and suffering are among the most apparent. The life of the early church was a demonstration of the life of Christ because the church shared the same kind of suffering he endured. The complementary teachings of Jesus and the apostles involving the meek and gentle character of his followers, the kind of love they are to show their enemies, and the non-use of physical force in dealing with evil, all assist in fulfilling the prophetic ministry and character of the church as the continuing witness and presence of the crucified body of Christ, the suffering agent of peace and reconciliation among men.

In the Old Testament literature, the coming Messiah is prophesied to be the champion of peace advocacy in having the title of Prince of Peace (Is. 9:6), and his kingdom is foreseen as a composition of people from many nations who forsake the tools of violence and force in favor of agricultural implements, symbols of non-threatening character and peace (Is. 2:1-4). Jesus taught that although his kingdom would be the victim of violence (Mat. 11:12), its citizens would not use physical force against people as do earthly kingdoms since neither the kingdom of God nor its citizens are of the world though they are in the world (Jn. 18:36).

In Messianic prophecy the chief advocate of peace, whose followers are to be a non-violent people, is himself the victim of physical abuse, rejection, and murder. "Although he had done no violence," the man of sorrows was "despised and rejected...stricken, smitten of God, and afflicted... wounded he was oppressed, yet when he was afflicted he did not open his mouth... he poured out his life unto death" (Is. 53). The prophetic picture of Jesus in his suffering is that he was as "a lamb before its shearers," that although he was the object of unjust attack, he made no attempt to resist by means of force or threats.

## *The Nature Of Meekness*

At the height of his ministry, Jesus taught his followers three principles that would insure the mission of the church as the suffering servant of reconciliation if indeed the church shaped its life accordingly. First, Jesus commended the character of meekness defined as gentleness in the face of wrath, patient and unresentful under injury and reproach, and this understanding of meek complements the other values of mercifulness and peace-making found among the beatitudes (Mat. 5: 5,7,9). The same essence of meekness is enjoined on Jesus' closest disciples who were commissioned to go as "sheep in the midst of wolves" and "harmless as doves" although they would be scourged, hated, and put to death. The warning to those who would be meek as Jesus taught, is that suffering at the hands of the evil oppressor is to be patiently endured unless a way of escape other than forcible resistance, is provided.

## *The Nature Of Love*

A second principle by which Jesus shapes the peaceable character of his people, involves the kind of love Christians are to show their enemies. The remarkable aspect of this love is that he who practices it, is willing to die for its object. In his first letter John writes, "This is how we know what love is: Jesus Christ laid down his life for us. And we ought to lay down our lives for our brothers" (I Jn. 3:16).

This is the love Jesus had for his enemies, for Paul asserts that God showed his love for us in that "while we were enemies, we were reconciled to God through the death of his son" (Rom. 5:10). This kind of selfless *agape* love is the love that Jesus showed in choosing to die rather than destroy his enemies. Loving one's enemies involves not only blessing, doing good to, and praying for them but also includes the readiness to be killed rather than to kill.

The event that makes the knowledge of this love especially new and relevant for the church, as opposed to love defined in the Old Testament, is the death of Christ. The love that God showed to us in the meek and dying Savior when we deserved to die because of our sin and hostility toward him, must be reflected in our lives as we relate even to our enemies who seek our injury and death.

We become real vessels of God's grace, only when we duplicate it in our relationships with people. If we fail to love our enemies as he did, we block the flow of grace and become barriers to the ministry of reconciliation. When we conduct ourselves as mirrors of his love in suffering non-resistantly and dying at the hands of his enemies, we join the company of the early church and of Paul who wrote, "We are always bearing about in the body the putting to death of Jesus, that the life also of Jesus may be manifested in our body. For we who live are always delivered unto death for Jesus' sake, that the life also of Jesus may be manifested in our mortal flesh" (II Cor. 4:10,11).

The dying of Jesus was in the non-resistant giving of himself in the place of his enemies, and as the early church practiced this same conduct in suffering, it became a testimony of the love, grace, and forgiveness which characterized the life of Jesus. In this way the church fulfills its mission as the suffering servant of peace and reconciliation. Seen in this light, the death of Jesus becomes the key to peace among men as well as peace with God.

## *Non-Resistance To Aggression*

The third concept that Jesus introduced was designed to give power to the meek as ministers of peace. He urged his followers to practice non-resistance before evil oppressors or assailants when he said, "Do not resist an evil person" (Mat. 5:39). James echoes this teaching in castigating the rich to whom he wrote, "You have condemned and murdered innocent men, who were not opposing you" (Jas. 5:6). Furthermore, the apostle Paul commended the Corinthians for their faithful practice of non-resistance when he wrote, "In fact, you even put up with anyone who enslaves you or exploits you or takes advantage of you or pushes himself forward or slaps you in the face" (II Cor. 11:20). Paul then, apparently referring to a particular incident in mind, admits that to his shame he had been too weak to practice non-resistance.

The result of faithful adherence to Jesus' teaching may be the injury or death of the righteous, yet this is the cost of discipleship.

Only this kind of radical ethic, calling for the non-use of force in dealing with evil, can empower the kingdom of God to become the real agent of peace and reconciliation.

## *The Church Under Attack*

As the church grew she began to encounter physically violent opposition. It is significant that Christians did not react to kill those who had killed their friends including their Savior, but they sought rather to imitate the conduct of Jesus in suffering. In their letters to the churches, the New Testament writers encouraged the early Christians to exhibit Christ-like conduct in suffering, and one's suffering at the hands of the opposition was cause for joy that the opportunity was given and that it was patiently endured (Acts 5:41).

Because of one's patient endurance in suffering, he was considered an heir of Christ and worthy to reign with him in his kingdom (Rom. 8:17,18; II Thess. 1:5). The act of suffering abuse was not commendable in itself, as later ascetics believed, but only if the victim suffered unjustly and non-resistantly, in meekness and love, as Jesus himself suffered.

## *The Example Of Hebrew Prophets*

Having mentioned the non-resistant death of the "righteous one" at the hands of wealthy tyrants, James exalts the example of the ancient prophets. "Brothers, as an example of patience in the face of suffering, take the prophets who spoke in the name of the Lord. As you know, we consider blessed those who have persevered" (Jas. 5:10,11). James ascribes happiness or blessedness to those who patiently endure suffering, and this is reminiscent of the beatitude of Jesus: "Blessed are you when people insult you, persecute you and falsely say all kinds of evil against you because of me. Rejoice and be glad, because great is your reward in heaven, for in the same way they persecuted the prophets who were before you" (Mat. 5:11,12). The early Christians were heirs of the ancient prophets in suffering and were encouraged to patiently endure as they did.

## *Not Only Religious Persecution*

The patient endurance of suffering is demonstrated as the proper mode of conduct for the Christian in the case of "religious" persecution, but Peter also encourages the practice of non-resistance for slaves who are beaten unjustly by their cruel masters and says that Christians are called to follow in the steps of Jesus: "He committed no sin, and no deceit was found in his mouth. When they hurled their insults at him, he did not retaliate; when he suffered, he made no threats. Instead, he entrusted himself to him who judges justly" (I Pet. 2:22,23).

Peter's statement allows us to suggest that patient endurance in suffering "religious" persecution is simply a specific application of the broader ethic of non-resistance stated in the Sermon on the Mount and elsewhere. The conduct of Jesus in suffering at the hands of the unrighteous is the example for Christians faced with the violence and oppression of evildoers. "But if you suffer for doing good and you endure it, this is commendable before God" (I Pet. 2:20).

## The First Christians Never Used Force

If the life and faith of the early church are considered exemplary for the modern church, biblical instances of Christians' use of physical force in dealing with evil become critical. Although the scriptures contain frequent mention of the use of physical force, the church is indicated to be the victim in every case. The biblical emphasis is therefore upon the blessedness of suffering patiently, the joy of sharing in the suffering of Christ, and the benefits of suffering faithfully. In no case were Christians advised to consider physical force as a means of dealing with the oppressive circumstances in which they lived. Paul observed in his letter to the Romans, "For your sake we face death all day long; we are considered as sheep to be slaughtered" (Rom. 8:36).

Elsewhere, Paul mentions his own patient suffering in persecution (I Cor. 4:12), which is in contrast to the period before his conversion when he was "a blasphemer and a persecutor and a violent man" (I Tim. 1:13) and that with legal sanction. Paul summarizes the completely one-sided nature of the persecution of the early church: "The son born in the ordinary way persecuted the son born by the power of the Spirit" (Gal. 4:29).

## *The Joy Of Suffering Unjustly*

The attitude of the early Christians in the midst of suffering is perhaps most frequently described as "joy." Peter and John rejoiced that they were counted worthy to suffer for Jesus (Acts 5:41). The letter to the Hebrews relates the joyful, non-resistant suffering of the Jewish Christians to whom he wrote, "Sometimes you were publicly exposed to insult and persecution; at other times you stood side by side with those who were so treated. You sympathized with those in prison and joyfully accepted the confiscation of your property, because you knew that you yourselves had better and lasting possessions" (Heb. 10: 33, 34). Suffering at the hands of evildoers identified the early Christians more closely with the sufferings of Christ, and this was cause for rejoicing. "But rejoice that you participate in the sufferings of Christ, so that you may be overjoyed when his glory is revealed" (I Pet. 4:13).

## Suffering As Jesus Did

This is a major concern of Peter who writes, "It is better, if it is God's will, to suffer for doing good than for doing evil. For Christ died for sins once for all, the righteous for the unrighteous" (I Pet. 3:17,18). The suffering of the righteous at the hands of the unrighteous is the calling of Christians, for this was the case with Jesus, and Christians are exhorted to "endure it" as Jesus did (I Pet. 2:20). In fact, Peter's view is that those who are willing to suffer physical abuse as Jesus did, have surely abandoned the practice of sin in their lives. "Therefore, since Christ suffered in his body, arm yourselves also with the same attitude, because he who has suffered in his body is done with sin" (I Pet. 4:1). Christians who justify the use of force in dealing with evil, cannot express their abandonment of sin to the ultimate degree of suffering non-resistantly.

## The Benefits Of Suffering As Christ Did

The non-resistant suffering of Christians at the hands of the unjust, resulted in several benefits. Not only does Christ-like suffering require and produce patience (Rom. 5:3,4), but also as mentioned earlier, through non-resistant suffering the Christian gives a testimony of the life and death of Jesus, of his love and forgiveness, and affirms that one is "done with sin" (I Pet. 4:1). Therefore, those who suffer patiently and faithfully are said to be worthy of the kingdom of God (II Thess.

1:5), eligible to reign with Christ (II Tim. 2:9,12), and "heirs of God and joint-heirs with Christ" (Rom. 8:17).

## The Christian Arsenal

The dynamic of Christ for overcoming evil and the world does not consist of weapons of physical force (I Jn. 5:4). The faith or gospel of Christ is the Christian's power to deal with all the forces of evil which seek to control the thoughts and actions of men. "The weapons we fight with are not the weapons of the world. On the contrary, they have divine power to demolish strongholds. We demolish arguments and every pretension that sets itself up against the knowledge of God, and we take captive every thought to make it obedient to Christ" (II Cor. 10:4,5). Those who are forced or threatened to obey an authority, are more likely to rebel than people whose every thought has been brought into captivity to the obedience of Christ, and for this reason the effectiveness of spiritual weapons is greater than that of physical weapons and warfare which are precluded by the meekness and gentleness of Christ in which his followers walk (II Cor. 10:1).

Christians who allow themselves to be drawn into war among nations, have misdirected and subverted their struggle, for "our wrestling is not against flesh and blood" (Eph. 6:12). The real war is for men's minds and souls and is directed "against the authorities, against the powers of this dark world and against the spiritual forces of evil in the heavenly realms" (Eph. 6:12).

Christians therefore must be willing to suffer physical abuse from their enemies, for spiritual weapons consist only of the gospel of peace, faith, truth, righteousness, salvation, and the word of God (Eph. 6:13-17). Other weapons that the Christian may employ are woven into his character and include love, kindness, meekness, and gentleness, which are to be shown toward all men. "Slander no one, be peaceable and considerate, and show meekness toward all men" (Tit. 3:2). Because of the importance of setting the proper example in relating to violent and evil persons, Paul is careful to prescribe for the prospective church leader that he should be "not violent but gentle" (I Tim. 3:3).

In the midst of physical abuse and suffering, the "servants of God" are equipped with "weapons of righteousness in the right hand and in the left" (II Cor. 6:3-10). Only these kinds of spiritual weapons that overcome evil with good (Rom. 12:21), are appropriate as the biblical dynamic by which the body of Christ fulfills its ministry as the agent of unity and reconciliation among men.

## Vulnerable But Not Powerless

Because of the nature of his weapons, the Christian is vulnerable to physical harm and death at the hands of the unrighteous, but this is the call and cost of discipleship to Christ. Although he is denied the use of physical force in dealing with evil, the Christian is not powerless, for showing kindness to his enemy is a way of heaping "burning coals on his head" (Rom. 12:20). Paul's suggestion to care for the physical needs of one's enemy is an example of how the Christian is expected to "overcome evil with good" (Rom. 12:21).

Aware of the plight of his readers, the writer to the Hebrews consoled them with the example of Jesus who also endured "opposition from sinful men," to the point of death on the cross. Likewise, the Hebrew Christians were expected to be faithful even to the shedding of their "own blood" (Heb. 12:2-4). The possibility of Christians shedding the blood of those who opposed them was not considered. This kind of suffering is to be endured as the chastening of God which is evidence to Christians that they are the sons of God and which benefits them by producing "a harvest of righteousness and peace for those who have been trained by it" (Heb. 12:11).

## Conversions Of Soldiers

Some aspects of the New Testament literature seem to clash with the central theme of the Christian's non-use of physical force in dealing with evil. Prior to their conversion, Cornelius and the Philippian jailer were government agents of force, and whether or not they continued to exercise the function of their positions is at most a matter of speculation. Supposing they understood the non-resistance ethic, the admonition to "love all men" as God loved them in the meek and dying Savior, and the primary exclusive ministry of Jesus' followers as agents of reconciliation, we must conclude that unless these principles and callings were suspended for them, these two men did not continue to exercise the full requirements of their civil positions. Rather, if Cornelius and the Philippian jailer were faithful and bold to confess the name and message of Jesus before men, they joined the ranks of the persecuted church and of the suffering Christ.

## *Jesus In The Temple*

During his ministry in Jerusalem, Jesus had occasion to enter the temple where merchants were selling animals for sacrifice and where others were changing foreign currency for profit. Jesus became enraged at the sight, and having made a whip, he drove out the animals and overturned the tables of the moneylenders. He accused them all of being thieves and of making "my Father's house into a market" (Jn. 2:16). Jesus' use of force in dealing with evil is undeniable, but whether or not this instance is an example for Christians is affected by two considerations: first, the Messianic prophecy, "zeal for your house consumes me" (Ps. 69:9), and second, the Jews recognized that just anyone could not do what Jesus did, without special authority, so they demanded of him, "What miraculous sign can you show us to prove your authority to do all this?" Jesus responded by giving them the sign of his resurrection: "Destroy this temple, and I will raise it again in three days" (Jn. 2: 13-22). Jesus' use of force in the temple was in fulfillment of prophecy and was for the purpose of focusing attention on his unique authority as the Messiah of God.

This instance is therefore not an example for Christians to follow and no scripture refers to it as such. Rather, Jesus' conduct in suffering and death is the example that biblical writers exhort Christians to imitate when faced with physical abuse at the hands of the unrighteous (I Pet. 2:20).

## Buy A Sword

The night of his arrest, Jesus told his apostles, "If you don't have a sword, sell your cloak and buy one" (Lk. 22:36). This appears to be in contradiction to Jesus' sending his apostles as "sheep among wolves" and "harmless as doves." The verses following Jesus' unusual request explains the rationale behind it. "It is written: 'and he was numbered with the transgressors'; and I tell you that this must be fulfilled in me" (Lk. 22:37). As they accompanied Jesus to his arrest, the apostles armed with swords would enable him to be "numbered with the transgressors" in fulfillment of Messianic prophecy (Is. 53:12).

When Jesus requested that his apostles take swords, he was perhaps already aware they were armed, for Jesus had warned them of his imminent death and they still hoped he would become the earthly king of a restored kingdom of Israel. Thus, when the apostles eager to defend Jesus readily presented two swords in response to Jesus' request, he indicated they would be enough to fulfill the prophecy. Later that evening, Peter who had refused to accept the necessity of Jesus' death, found occasion to use one of the swords by cutting off the ear of a servant of the high priest. Jesus quickly said, "No more of this!" and the prophecy was fulfilled with Peter himself among the lawless with whom Jesus was numbered. Again, as in the cleansing of the temple, the act of violence on the betrayal night is not an example for Christians to follow, but rather the conduct of Jesus in his suffering, which began on that night, is for the imitation of all Christians.

## Government Is Established By God

In his letter to the Christians at Rome, the apostle Paul briefly defines the purpose of civil government and describes the responsibilities of Christians in relation to it. Paul explains that God establishes every government for the purpose of maintaining order in society by means of physical force. The Christian's responsibilities to civil government include behaving in an orderly manner in society, paying taxes as Jesus also commanded, and giving due respect to government officials (Rom. 13:1-7). None of these responsibilities imply that a Christian may serve in the capacity of ruler or agent of force.

Characteristically, all earthly governments regardless of their political forms and philosophies, share the common function of acting as the regulators of order within society by means of physical force and threats of force. Citizens who cause disorder by stealing, murder, assault, and similar acts are threatened with various forms of punishment such as imprisonment, fines, or execution. The disorderly person is made to suffer for his "sins," and God's purpose to avenge evil is accomplished whether or not the government is cognizant of God or his divine purpose. Thus, it can be said that God establishes every government, by virtue of its inherent ends and means in the ruling process, in that it serves his ultimate purposes. However, when governments present opportunities or extend citizen responsibilities beyond that which is appropriate for the Christian, the latter must decline participation and endure the consequences.

## *The Unique Christian Calling*

The appropriateness of the Christian's participation in the ruling process, the judicial system, and war against nations, must be considered in the light of one's unique and primary calling as a member of the suffering body of Christ. In the case of war, national interests and loyalties are elevated above the international spiritual bond, and Christians who participate are compelled to substitute a national view of the church for the biblical global view. Thus, in war the ministry of the church to reconcile all people to God and to each other in the unity of the body of Christ, is rendered meaningless unless Christians abstain from war and remain faithful to their calling.

The ruling process is itself anti-thetical to the unique calling of Christians who deal with evil through their spiritual warfare as opposed to the physical coercive means employed by governments. Because the democratic form of government as we know it, did not exist during the period of the early church, it remains for modern Christians to make new application of the non-use-of-force ethic.

## *The Majority Rules By Threat Of Force*

Through the voting process, a majority of enfranchised citizens choosing to vote, express their collective will, with the clear understanding that their decision is enforced upon the entire population through various laws with penalties attached for their violation. Through elected representatives, the majority exercises ruling power over the minority and thus becomes part of the mechanism of legitimized force and violence which is the prerogative of civil government. This is government, or rule, by and of the people.

Theoretically, the majority rules with the consent of minority and protecting minority rights, but in reality many elements including those born into society and minority groups within society have not given consent to the laws that convict or oppress them. When Christians vote they become part of the ruling process in which minority interests are often over-ruled. With the protection of the constitution by means of courts, police, military force, guns, and prisons, the will of the majority prevails by threats of force made against anyone who would violate that will. Therefore, by force and threat of force, the rule of the majority is maintained and implemented. For citizens of the kingdom of God, an arsenal of spiritual weapons to further the purposes of reforming man's nature and actions has replaced the use of coercive force.

## The Plaintiff Seeks Use Of Force

Through the judicial system, people who have been wronged or injured by others may seek recompense. In this process, the plaintiff or injured party brings legal charges against his offending enemy in a court of law, and in so doing the plaintiff is asking the government to exercise force or the threat of force against the defendant charged with the trespass. If the matter is decided in favor of the plaintiff, the court issues an order against the defendant that will involve a sentence of imprisonment, fine payment, or death carried out by force.

If found guilty of the charges, the defendant may appeal to a higher court, and in so doing he is asking the government to reconsider its threats of force against him. The defendant is not in a position to ask the court to exercise force against the plaintiff unless the defendant wishes to enter legal charges against him in a counter-claim or in a separate case and assumes the role of plaintiff. This understanding of the modern legal process, is essential for a consideration of the Christian's proper role in court.

The New Testament literature suggests that the ethic of non-resistance should be extended to preclude a Christian's pressing legal charges against anyone in civil court. In his first letter to the Corinthians, Paul contends that legal problems among Christians should be decided by the church rather than by unbelieving court officials. But more than that, for Christians to have lawsuits among themselves at all was fundamentally wrong. "The very fact that you have lawsuits among you means you have been completely defeated already. Why not rather be wronged? Why not rather be cheated?" (I Cor. 6:7).

The moral high ground is to be wronged and cheated rather than go to court. If the Corinthian Christians had not yet learned to refrain from civil lawsuits among themselves, they would have even more difficulty learning not to use the courts to coerce unbelieving neighbors. Persecution was not widespread in this period, and Christians would have had access to the judicial system. Although Paul's reference is sarcastic in the second letter to the Corinthians, nonetheless they had learned from his first letter to prefer being wronged and cheated rather than take anyone to court (II Cor. 11:20), and this is truly the spirit of non-resistance.

## Paul Brought No Legal Charges

Another case in point involves the apostle Paul who was the object of a murder conspiracy organized by a group of forty Jews. Following a public riot that resulted when Asiatic Jews incited a crowd in Jerusalem to kill Paul, he was arrested by Roman authorities who were prepared to interrogate him by flogging. He informed them that he was a Roman citizen and that it was illegal for them to flog him. In referring to his rights as a Roman citizen, Paul both saved himself from harm and prevented the Roman officials from breaking the law. There is however no implication that Paul would have brought legal charges against the officials (Acts 21:27-22:29).

Pending further investigation of his case, the apostle Paul remained under arrest and in the custody of a military commander who kept Paul surrounded by a detachment of soldiers. During this time, a group of forty Jews conspired with the chief priests to kill Paul. The plan was for the Sanhedrin to petition the commander to send Paul to them on the pretext of wanting more accurate information about his case, and on the way to Jerusalem the Jews intended to ambush and kill Paul. Fortunately, Paul's nephew overheard the plot and informed Paul who then sent the youth to inform the commander. The nephew explained the plot to the commander and simply asked him not to give in to the Jews' request to send Paul to the Sanhedrin. Again, it is significant that Paul and his nephew neither pressed legal charges against the conspiring Jews nor suggested that the commander use his troops to arrest or otherwise deal with the conspirators by force where they were hiding (Acts 23:10-35).

Still under arrest and in military custody, Paul was transferred under heavy guard to governor Felix in Caesarea where the Jews brought charges against Paul. Two years passed and Paul then appeared before Festus who wanted to do the Jews a favor by sending the apostle to Jerusalem where they planned to kill him. But Paul appealed his case to Caesar, and in so doing he later declared to have had no charges to bring against the Jews (Acts 28:19).

Throughout his court involvements over a lengthy period of time, Paul was severely mistreated and threatened, yet he never called upon the government or court to take plaintiff action against his accusers. Paul's conduct at the hands of his evil oppressors was enjoined upon the Corinthians (I Cor. 6:7) and is consistent with the non-resistance ethic demonstrated in every biblical instance in which Christians were confronted with the forces of evil in society.

## *The Early Church Before Augustine*

The non-violence position among the early post-apostolic church writers until the fourth century is significant in reflecting the universality of its acceptance in the church and because of the biblical reasons used by the early church writers. The similarity of the early Christian view in the second century with that of the biblical record is such that a representative sample from the early post-apostolic treatises will serve to summarize the major points of our thesis.

The non-resistant suffering and death of the innocent Saviour at the hands of his enemies was foremost in the minds of those early Christians. His example gave new meaning to love and provided an important rationale for the practice of non-violence.

## *Ignatius of Antioch*

"And let us imitate the Lord, 'who, when he was reviled, reviled not again'; when he was crucified, He said, 'Father, forgive them, they know not what they do.' If anyone, the more he is injured, displays the more patience, blessed is he" (Ignatius of Antioch, 80-140 A.D., *Epistle to the Ephesians*). As we have seen from scripture, this kind of suffering elicited joy from the early Christians, and they were encouraged to be meek and patient as a testimony of the life and death, love and forgiveness, of Christ himself. To endure suffering as Jesus endured is to suffer for his sake because the testimony of Christ is in such suffering.

Also, in writing to the Ephesians, Ignatius refers to the Christian's proper weapons in confrontations with the abusive forces of evil. "Be humble in response to their wrath... Conquer their harsh temper by gentleness and meekness... Wherefore Paul exhorts as follows: And the Lord's servant must not quarrel; instead, he must be kind to everyone, able to teach, not resentful. Those who oppose him he must gently instruct, in the hope that God will grant them repentance leading them to a knowledge of the truth" (II Tim. 2:24, 25).

## *Tertullian and Athenagoras*

Among the early church writers, the "resist not" statement in the Sermon on the Mount was regarded as a major premise of the non-resistance ethic and was directly related to prohibitions against Christians' going to court as plaintiffs or to war against anyone. Notice also the allusions to prophecies regarding the Messianic kingdom and to the unique and primary calling of Christians to the ministry of reconciliation.

In the context of a defense of Christian pacifism Tertullian argues, "Shall the son of peace take part in the battle when it does not become him even to sue at law?" (200 A.D., *On the Crown*) Corroborating Paul's description of the Corinthians (II Cor. 11:20), Athenagoras shows the general understanding among Christians was against their taking plaintiff action: "We have learned not only not to return blow for blow, nor to go to law with those who plunder and rob us, but to those who smite us on one side of the face to offer the other side also..." (177 A.D., *A Plea for Christians*).

## *Justin Martyr and Ireneaus*

Justin Martyr believed the church was the literal fulfillment of Isaiah's kingdom prophecy (Is. 2:1-4). "We who were filled with war and mutual slaughter and every wickedness, have each through the whole earth changed our war-like weapons, our swords into plowshares and our spears into implements of tillage, and we cultivate piety, righteousness, philanthropy, faith and hope..." (150 A.D., *Dialogue with Trypho*).

Irenaeus concurred with this and also related the prophetic fulfillment to Jesus' instructions concerning non-resistance. "But if the law of liberty, that is, the word of God, preached by the apostles.... Caused such a change in the state of things, that these nations did form the war-lances into plowshares... that is into instruments used for peaceful purposes... and when smitten offer also the other cheek..." (183 A.D., *Against Heresies*).

## *Origen and Hippolytus*

Origen bases his anti-war stand upon the church as being the literal fulfillment of Isaiah's prophecy and as having a unique ministry of peace. "We no longer take up 'sword against nation' nor do we 'learn war anymore' having become children of peace for the sake of Jesus who is our leader" (225 A.D., *Against Celsus*).

Celsus was a pagan critic of Christianity who recognized that non-violence was the common practice among Christians. He commented, "If everyone should do the same as you, nothing would prevent the emperor from being left alone and deserted, and the affairs of the whole earth would come into the hands of the most lawless and wildest barbarians" (*Against Celsus*). Origen did not deny Celsus' fear that if everyone became Christian the emperor would be left alone to rule, but Origen's reply was that Christians "recognize in each city another native constitution, created by the word of God... Christians decline public offices not in order to escape these duties but in order to keep themselves for a more divine and necessary service in the church of God for the salvation of men" (*Against Celsus*). Origen recognized the unique mission and calling of the kingdom of God and believed this precludes Christians participating in the ruling processes of worldly kingdoms.

For Hippolytus the application of non-violence is precise and includes prohibitions of a Christian's becoming a soldier, ruler, or judge. "A soldier of the government must be told not to execute men; if he shall be ordered to do it, he shall not do it. He must be told not to take the military oath. If he will not agree, let him be rejected (from baptism). A military governor or a magistrate of a city who wears the purple, either let him desist or let him be rejected. If a catechumen or a baptized Christian wishes to become a soldier, let him be cast out. For he has despised God..." (220 A.D., *Apostolic Tradition*). Tertullian had earlier found similar occupations to be inconsistent with the Christian walk when he wrote, "And shall he apply the chain and the prison and the torture and the punishment, who is not the avenger even of his own wrongs?" (*On the Crown*).

The radical ethic of non-violence with its many social and political implications, was fervently espoused by the church for several centuries and marked her as a living testimony of the crucified Christ. Like nearly all radical movements, the church eventually came to terms with the dominant culture and began to reflect the comfortable socially constructed values rather than the more costly realities of the kingdom of God.

In the fourth century, the Roman emperor Constantine united cross and sword at Milvan Bridge in his well-publicized "vision of the cross" with the words "In This Sign Conquer." Who remembered his previous vision of Apollos that served his political and military purposes?

The church became militarized and politicized. To accommodate the mass conversion of Roman ruling parties and the general populace, Augustine of Hippo in the fifth century, formulated the just war doctrine still accepted today by Protestant and Roman Catholic followers.

Despite the obvious compromise, modern Christians have integrated discipleship to Christ with cultural practices and sentiments. Divine values of gentleness, meekness, and love must now compete with the popular appetite for violence and brutality in the media and with the patriotic zeal surrounding military campaigns and the rhetoric of political freedom.

In every generation and for the effective continuation of the Messianic kingdom, the dynamic power of the suffering Saviour must be clearly presented and urged upon his followers if they would be truly light and salt in the world.

# 6

# *Peacemaking In Action: How To Manage Conflict*

The contents of this chapter have been used in training counselors and in helping groups and individuals experiencing conflict. Understanding that emotions often complicate the process and can be addressed through various sub-skills, the same general principles for resolving conflict between individuals may be transferable to conflict in organizations and between nations. These principles can be summarized as follows:

1. asserting the issues
2. listening to and reflecting the issues
3. problem-solving the issues

## *You Can't Avoid It*

Conflict is something that cannot be avoided no matter how hard we try. Conflict is inevitable because people are individuals with different views, feelings, experiences, and ways of perceiving things. While not all conflict can be resolved, the object is not to eliminate conflict but to try to work with conflict so that it is most likely to have a positive outcome, such as mutual acceptance, bringing people closer, or creating new ideas and new possibilities.

## *Unidentified Flying Patterns*

Individual styles of communication and conflict may spring from earlier experiences and influences unknown to those involved. Those experiences are a major part of life patterns that often come from a dysfunctional family of origin, maybe from unresolved conflict in the parental relationships from childhood, or from significant unresolved losses. These unhealthy and often unconscious patterns of communication block one's ability to resolve conflict and also serve to repeat and perpetuate past unresolved conflicts and losses.

An individual may be overly passive or overly aggressive, or a combination of those behaviours. Ways of relating are unintentional, unconscious compulsions, and often one is unaware of healthy alternatives to reacting out of emotion or habit. There are five basic communication styles: passive, aggressive, passively aggressive, destructive, and assertive.

## *Who Is The Passive Person?*

The passive style tries to avoid a conflict and tends to be agreeable. Emotions and opinions are often hidden, and so it is hard to get to know the passive individual. This person may behave as a doormat and may apologize prematurely. He avoids conflict at all cost and wants to keep things nice. Eye contact is averted and body language may appear as a lowered head or slouching in his seat for example.

The person who has a passive style is behaving as if he does not believe that he has worth equal to others. He behaves as if he is not entitled to his own feelings and views, and as if he is not entitled to be treated with respect. If you call him names or put him down, he will not stand up for his right to be treated with respect. He may put his head down, or tuck his tail between his legs, so to speak. He may even agree with the person who labels him or calls him names. He may also make self-demeaning comments such as calling himself stupid.

## *Look Out For the Aggressive Person!*

This is a pushy style, loud and dominating. The person with this style wants what he wants, and he may order you to get it for him or do it for him. He is demanding and obnoxious.

So he may accuse, blame other people, and point his finger. The aggressive individual behaves as if he alone has worth, and you do not. He behaves as if he alone is to be treated with respect, but he treats you with disrespect. He behaves as if only he is entitled to his feelings and views, so he dominates the time. He interrupts you if you are talking and leaves little space for your point of view. He insists that he is right and you are wrong.

Deep down the aggressive individual is very insecure and afraid and has low self worth. He has very low ego strength. If he had a stronger sense of himself, he would feel less compelled to be controlling and dominating.

## Passively Aggressive, Indirectly Speaking

A variation on aggressive style is passively aggressive style, which is demonstrated by the indirect or passive expression of hostility. Passive resistance is passive aggression. Deliberately burning the toast at breakfast as an expression of resentment, is an example.

Sabotaging, undermining, talking about people behind their backs are all passive aggressive behaviours. This person does not verbalize his emotions directly, especially anger. He may use a punitive silence, or refuse to speak to someone for a long period of time. The cold shoulder is passive aggressive, as also is walking away from a person when he is talking or yawning in his face or talking to others as a way of excluding him, instead of directly verbalizing the anger.

## Avoid The Destructive Person If You Can

Destructive style is characterized by hitting, throwing objects, name-calling, threats, yelling and screaming. It includes physical behaviour that is destructive of property or of a person's body, as well as verbal behaviour intended to destroy a person's value or self-worth such as name-calling and judgmental terms to demean a person.

Sarcastic put downs are destructive because they imply a label of stupidity, ignorance or weakness; for example, saying, "Where were you when they passed out the brains?"

This type of behaviour and other unhealthy styles may have their origin in very dysfunctional parenting where there was physical or mental violence, sexual abuse, or lack of discipline.

## *Aim For Assertiveness*

The assertive style and ability to raise issues in an assertive way, are most effective in resolving conflict. Assertiveness is being able to be clear, direct, brief, and non-judgmental. The assertive individual behaves as if he believes everyone is entitled to his or her feelings and views. He believes, "You're entitled to your view, and I'm entitled to my view," and therefore he is *brief*. He states his case but he wants to know your point of view as well. He gives you equal time. He is *clear* about his feelings, and he says what he feels using feeling words. Some examples are: "I feel annoyed, I feel sad, I feel afraid."

When he describes your behaviour he is able to use *non-judgmental* terms. He's just going to state a non-judgmental description of your observable behaviour. An assertive example of this is saying, "When you don't take accurate phone messages, I can't return calls." He does not call the person derogatory names but stays with what he observes and states the effect on his life.

## *Where Do Unhealthy Patterns Come From?*

Regarding the development of these styles, some of the unhealthy communication patterns and the destructive styles are modeled on what was experienced in the family of origin, and some are a reaction against styles and experiences in the family of origin. Some researchers believe basic styles are present at birth and observe that babies are often generally easy or difficult.

If in the family of origin there was violence, a person may reject the expression of anger as only destructive, so he develops a passive style to keep his anger in. Then he has explosive outbursts at times because if he keeps his anger in about things, the tension may build to the point that he spews out name-calling or other destructive behaviours. This reconfirms to him that anger is no good so he stuffs it all again and goes through the cycle.

If a person grows up with two passive parents who avoided conflict and then he finds a partner who is very aggressive, he will lack skills because when he was growing up he did not observe conflict or strong anger managed in any constructive way. Someone who grew up with both passive and aggressive styles in the same family may be capable of both passive and aggressive styles - both the doormat and the bully.

A goal in self-awareness is to understand the story behind one's style and then to develop a broad repertoire of styles and skills for communicating and dealing with conflict.

## Three Primary Skills

In developing a broad repertoire of healthy styles and skills for communication and conflict resolution, there are three primary areas of focus. The first skill is expressing feelings and views in a more assertive way, eliminating threats, name-calling and judgmental terms. The second skill is listening to the feelings and views of the other person. Thirdly, problem solving skills lead directly to reaching an agreement without taking power or controlling. Both the aggressive style and passive style are very controlling and power-seeking.

## Give Up The Power

The passive individual may, in an unhealthy way, be very powerful in his use of silence and other passive aggressive behaviours. And the aggressive person in his unhealthy way tends to be very powerful by demanding, ordering, and intimidating people. If we want to help a person give up power and move beyond control in relationships, we need to help him learn new healthy skills.

## *Let's Get Assertive!*

Expressing issues fully about relationships past and present, is important. Taking care of unfinished business is essential in grief counseling, and the same principle applies to resolving or addressing conflicts in relationships.

In developing assertiveness skills, a simple formula is the three-part assertive statement, which is: "I feel _____, when you _____, because _____." In the first blank, put in a feeling word such as: annoyed, sad, afraid, frustrated, angry, or irritated. Choose a word that matches the kind or level of emotion. In the "when you" blank, provide a non-judgmental description of observable behaviour. In the "because" blank, clarify the effect on your life resulting from the other person's behaviour.

Here are some examples of assertive statements:
"I feel frustrated when you don't put gas in the tank and leave it on empty because then I have to stop by the gas station to fill the tank, and I'm late for work."

"I feel really cheated when you don't follow through on the tasks we agreed that you would do because then I'm left with more work."

"I feel frustrated when you don't phone to let me know you are going to be late because then I lose valuable time waiting."

In some situations or cultures it may work best to leave out the emotion or "I feel" part of the assertive statement. The word "angry" or other feeling words may trigger a defensive reaction, so one may try using just the last two parts of the assertive statement: "When you_____, then I _____." For example, "When you don't take out the trash as you agreed, it makes more work for me."

## What Are The Barriers?

The passive person struggles with fear and guilt when he attempts to become assertive. The fear is about hurting or being hurt, of saying something that they fear will hurt the other person, or of experiencing a negative reaction from the other person. When the feared thing happens, he feels guilty and responsible. The end result is the *protection syndrome:* avoiding conflict or excusing the other person or apologizing unnecessarily.

The passive individual prefers to avoid stating the issue clearly. He might allude to it, probably in vague and general ways. What the passive person needs to understand is that passivity, or any one of the other styles of communicating except the destructive style, might be appropriate in a given situation. The bottom line is to choose the style as a conscious, deliberate decision, rather than as an impulsive reaction. For instance, if one is talking with a policeman or an employer, one may wisely choose to be passive or even apologetic.

## *Listen To Their Issues*

Another essential skill is the reflective listening statement. This can be easily remembered as the opposite of the assertive statement.

The formula for the reflective statement is: "So you feel _____ when I _____ because_____." Then simply add a perception check at the end: "Is that what you're feeling?" "Is that what you're saying?" or "Do I understand you?"

Essentially, with the reflective statement the listener reflects the emotion of the person who is upset, the behaviour he is upset about, and how his life is affected. It is more effective for the listener to overstate than to understate the person who is speaking. In other words, when the listener makes a reflective statement, it is best to reflect somewhat more than the speaker has said including the implications of what the speaker has said supporting the speakers position. The listener reflects in a way that sincerely advocates and supports the feelings and views of the speaker. This is a key to reducing tension in a conflict situation and preventing escalation.

Often the speaker does not say what the practical effect is on his life. He only points out the disturbing behaviour. In that case, when one makes a reflection, one reflects how his behaviour has affected the other person's life, even if they have not stated it, in order to help them feel fully understood. This is important *before* asserting one's own issues or point of view.

In a conflict, it is important to exchange a series of reflective statements. Use reflections to clarify the issues to be resolved, and if the other person does not know about reflective listening, and most often they do not, one can still elicit a reflection in order to feel understood by the other party. You can do this by saying, "What do you hear me saying?" or "Let me know what you think you heard me say, because I need to know that you understood what I've said, so we can go further. I need to know that you understand my point of view."

The first step to resolving conflict is to ensure the issues are clear to each party. Then one can begin to problem solve.

## What About Fighting?

A conflict may degenerate into a fight or argument. The definition of a fight is when one person is unwilling to listen to the point of view of the other. And it only takes one person who is unwilling to listen to the point of view of the other to have a fight. It could be a silent fight or a verbal fight. One could use a wall of words to keep from listening to the other or one could use a wall of silence.

It's very important for fighting behaviour to be recognized early on, and there are two things one can do to manage it. The first is to keep the fight fair by setting guidelines. As long as there are no threats, name-calling, put-downs, or physical anger, the fight is within fair limits.

The second way to manage fighting is to recognize that as much as the parties may want to resolve the issue, they may be too emotionally wound up to begin to be reasonable at all. At those times it's very important to say: "I can't talk about this now, but I'll talk about it this evening or when I think I'm ready to talk about it." If the other person is refusing to talk, or after a period of distance, it is important to come back to the other party and say, "I'm ready to talk about this if you are." At that time the parties can sit down and make assertive and reflective statements.

## *Problem Solving Is The Most Fun*

Clarify the issues and then move it to the next step, which is to say: "What are we going to do? What are some possible solutions?" This question helps to move to the problem-solving phase, which is essential to the resolution of the conflict. One must get around to saying: "What are we going to do about your issue, about our issue, about my issue?"

At that point one can begin to problem solve. To use a very structured approach to problem solving, get pencils and separate sheets of paper and *make a list* of the issues of each party and then prioritize them. For example: "I'll circle my most important issue, and you'll circle yours. We'll flip a coin to see whose issue gets dealt with first."

Take that issue and start *brainstorming* solutions. For this, write the issue on a sheet of paper, then each person verbally proposes different possible solutions or ideas even ideas that sound far-fetched allowing for creativity. Brainstorming must be done by immediately listing whatever solution is suggested without discussion or argument.

When seven or more solutions are listed and numbered for a problem, each party privately chooses two or three that he or she believes would work best to solve the problem. Finally, the parties compare solutions by circling their choices. The agreement is found where the parties overlap in their choice of solutions. All that remains is to agree on a time frame to implement the solution. If an agreed solution does not work, go back through the problem-solving process again.

## *Structure Is The Key*

This is a very structured problem-solving process. Structure is the key to maintaining safety in conflict, especially if the conflict is emotionally intense and there are multiple, confusing issues to be dealt with. In this case it is most helpful to use a written process. One also needs to give the emotions time to settle, because when people try to resolve things too early, they get bogged down and begin to react emotionally to things that are said.

## *Remember These Biblical Principles*

- A soft answer reduces the other person's strong anger (Proverbs 15:1).
- Be soon to listen, slow to speak and slow to become angry (James 1:19).
- Resolve conflict as soon as possible. Do not let the sun go down while you are still angry (Ephesians 4:26).

- Reach an agreement with your opponent before he takes you to court (Matthew 5:25).
- Be patient and not quick tempered (Proverbs 14:29).
- Overreacting in anger will increase conflict whereas waiting in silence can calm the hostility (Proverbs 15:18).
- Avoid name-calling completely (Matthew 5:22).
- Do not retaliate physically when hit, pushed or spat upon (Matthew 5:39).
- The use of judgmental terms will result in the other person judging you in return (Matthew 7:1).
- Never be vindictive nor try to get back at the other person (Romans 12:19).
- Use someone wise to help mediate a dispute (I Corinthians 6:1-6).
- Get rid of all bitterness, rage, anger, and malice (Ephesians 4:31).
- Be tolerant and forgiving of grievances (Colossians 3:13).

Accept the fact that resolving conflict may not be easy, and sometimes it may not be possible. Your willingness to remain open to the other person's point of view and your willingness to forgive and to ask for forgiveness, are essential to healing and reconciliation.

# 7

# *The Peaceable Kingdom: A Bible Concordance for Pacifists*

**Words and Scriptures with Commentary Relating to the Christian's Conduct Toward His Enemies**

*It shall come to pass in the latter days that the mountain of the house of the LORD shall be established as the highest of the mountains, and shall be raised above the hills; and all the nations shall flow to it, and many peoples shall come, and say: "Come, let us go up to the mountain of the LORD, to the house of the God of Jacob; that he may teach us his ways and that we may walk in his paths." For out of Zion shall go forth the law, and the word of the LORD from Jerusalem. He shall judge between the nations, and shall decide for many peoples; and they shall beat their swords into plowshares, and their spears into pruning hooks; nation shall not lift up sword against nation, neither shall they learn war any more.*                                        *Isaiah 2:2-4*

*There shall come forth a shoot from the stump of Jesse, and a branch shall grow out of his roots. And the Spirit of the LORD shall rest upon him, the spirit of wisdom and understanding, the spirit of counsel and might, the spirit of knowledge and the fear of the LORD. And his delight shall be in the fear of the LORD. He shall not judge by what his eyes see, or decide by what his ears hear; but with righteousness he shall judge the poor, and decide with equity for the meek of the earth; and he shall smite the earth with the rod of his mouth, and with the breath of his lips he shall slay the wicked. Righteousness shall be the girdle of his waist, and faithfulness the girdle of his loins. The wolf shall dwell with the lamb, and the leopard shall lie down with the kid, and the calf and the lion and the fatling together, and a little child shall lead them. The cow and the bear shall feed; their young shall lie down together; and the lion shall eat straw like the ox. The sucking child shall play over the hole of the asp, and the weaned child shall put his hand on the adder's den. They shall not hurt or destroy in all my holy mountain.*                  *Isaiah 11:1-9*

# Table of Contents

1. Adversary
2. Affliction
3. Armour
4. Beat
5. Bless
6. Bonds
7. Chasten
8. Compassion
9. Court of law
10. Death
11. Destroy
12. Do Good
13. Endurance
14. Enemy
15. Evil
16. Fight
17. Force
18. Forgiveness
19. Gentleness
20. Harmless
21. Hate
22. Honor
23. Humility
24. Kill
25. Kindness
26. Longsuffering
27. Love
28. Lowliness
29. Meekness
30. Mercy
31. Overcome
32. Patience
33. Peace
34. Persecution
35. Plunder
36. Recompense
37. Reproach
38. Resist
39. Revile
40. Smite
41. Stoned
42. Strike
43. Stripes
44. Suffering
45. Threaten
46. Tribulation
47. Terror
48. Vengeance
49. Violence
50. War
51. Weapons

**1. Adversary/Adversity**

Jesus urges us to resolve conflicts with our opponents before legal force is used against us. In the face of persecution, we should not be frightened by anything our adversaries can do to us because we are confident that God will save us in heaven when we die. Christians do not need to use physical force in defense. Young widows, as well as all Christians, should live in holiness so that enemies cannot make accusations of bad conduct. God will punish our enemies after this life, and so there is no need for us to seek their punishment. We should have such empathy for those who suffer persecution that we feel we are suffering with them.

Matt. 5:25 - Agree with your adversary quickly, while you are in the way with him; before the adversary delivers you to the judge, and the judge delivers you to the officer, and you be cast into prison.
Phil. 1:28 - And in nothing terrified by your adversaries: which is to them an evident token of perdition, but to you of salvation, and that of God.
I Tim. 5:14 - I will therefore that the younger women marry, bear children, guide the house, give none occasion to the adversary to speak reproachfully.
Heb. 10:27 - But a certain fearful looking for of judgment and fiery indignation, which shall devour the adversaries.

Heb. 13:3 - Remember those who... suffer adversity, as being yourselves also in the body.

**2. Affliction**

The scripture consistently describes Jesus' followers as victims of violence rather than perpetrators of violence. The example of the apostles and of other Christians suffering affliction encourages us to endure affliction and to rejoice in affliction.

Matt. 24:9 – the shall they deliver you up to be afflicted
Mk. 4:17 – when affliction or persecution arises for the word's sake
Acts 20:23 – the Holy Spirit witnesses in every city, saying that bonds and afflictions await me
II Cor. 1:6 – And whether we be afflicted, it is for your consolation and salvation, which is effectual in the enduring of the same sufferings which we also suffer
II Cor. 6:4 – But in all things approving ourselves as the ministers of God, in much patience, in afflictions
II Cor. 8:2 – How that in a great trial of affliction the abundance of their joy
I Thess. 1:6 – And you became followers of us, and of the Lord, having received the word in much affliction, with joy
I Thess. 3:3 – That no man should be moved by these afflictions: for yourselves know that we are appointed to this

I Thess. 3:7 – Therefore, brethren, we were comforted over you in all our affliction and distress by your faith

II Tim. 1:8 – be a partaker of the afflictions of the gospel

II Tim. 3:11 – Persecutions, afflictions, which came unto me at Antioch, at Iconium, at Lystra

II Tim. 4:5 – endure afflictions

Heb. 10:32 – you endured a great fight of afflictions

Heb. 10:33 - you were made a gazingstock both by reproaches and afflictions; and partly, while you became companions of them that were so used

James 5:10 – Take, my brethren, the prophets, who have spoken in the name of the Lord, for an example of suffering affliction, and of patience.

I Pet. 5:9 - Whom resist firmly in the faith, knowing that the same afflictions are accomplished in your brethren that are in the world.

### 3. Armour

The scriptures consistently describe the Christian armour, weaponry, and struggle in spiritual terms rather than physical terms. The Christian struggle is "not against flesh and blood."

Rom. 13:12 - The night is almost gone, the day is at hand: let us therefore throw off the works of darkness, and let us put on the armour of light.

II Cor. 6:7 - By the word of truth, by the power of God, by the armour of righteousness on the right hand and on the left

Eph. 6:11-17 - Put on the whole armour of God, that you may be able to stand against the wiles of the devil. For we wrestle not against flesh and blood, but against principalities, against powers, against the rulers of the darkness of this world, against spiritual wickedness in high places. For this reason, take for yourselves the whole armour of God, that you may be able to withstand in the evil day, and having done all, to stand. Stand therefore, having your waist covered with truth, and having on the breastplate of righteousness; and your feet with shoes made of the gospel of peace. Above all, take the shield of faith, whereby you shall be able to quench all the fiery darts of the wicked. And take the helmet of salvation, and the sword of the Spirit, which is the word of God

I Thess. 5:8 - But let us, who are of the day, be sober, putting on the breastplate of faith and love; and for a helmet, the hope of salvation.

## 4. Beat

The early Christians were only victims of beating and never engaged in or condoned the beating of others.

Mark 13:9 - But be aware of this, for they shall deliver you up to councils; and in the synagogues you shall be beaten

Acts 5:40 - And to him they agreed: and when they had called the apostles, and beaten them, they commanded that they should not speak in the name of Jesus, and let them go.

Acts 16:22 - And the multitude rose up together against them: and the magistrates tore their clothes, and commanded to beat them.

Acts 16:37 - But Paul said to them, They have beaten us openly uncondemned, being Romans, and have cast us into prison

Acts 21:32 - Who immediately took soldiers and centurions, and ran down to them: and when they saw the chief captain and the soldiers, they stopped beating Paul.

Acts 22:19 - And I said, Lord, they know that I imprisoned and beat in every synagogue those who believed on you

II Cor. 11:25 – Three times was I beaten with rods, once was I stoned

## 5. Bless

Disciples are called to bless their enemies whenever attacked verbally or physically and are blessed and encouraged to rejoice when they suffer in this way. The reward for those so treated is a heavenly blessing.

Matt. 5:3-11 - Blessed are the meek, merciful, peacemakers, the persecuted for righteousness' sake.

Matt. 5:44 - Bless them that curse you

Lk. 6:22 - Blessed are you, when men shall hate you, ... separate you, ... reproach you, and cast out your name as evil, for the Son of man's sake.

Lk. 6:28 - Bless them that curse you

Rom. 12:14 - Bless them which persecute you: bless, and curse not.

I Cor. 4:12 - being reviled, we bless

I Pet. 3:9 - Not rendering evil for evil, or railing for railing: but on the contrary, blessing; knowing that you are called to this, that you should inherit a blessing.

## 6. Bonds/Bound

God's people were arrested or placed in bonds but never sought the arrest of others or for others to be placed in bonds or in prison.

Acts 9:2 – if he found any of this Way, whether they were men or women, he might bring them bound to Jerusalem

Acts 21:13 - Then Paul answered, What do you mean to weep and to break my heart? For I am ready not to be bound only, but also to die at Jerusalem for the name of the Lord Jesus.

Acts 21:33 - Then the chief captain came near, and took him, and commanded him to be bound with two chains; and demanded whom he was, and what he had done.

Acts 22:4 - And I persecuted this way unto the death, binding and delivering into prisons both men and women.

II Cor. 11:20 – you allow it, if anyone puts bonds on you
Eph. 6:20 – for which I am an ambassador in bonds
II Tim. 2:9 – wherein I suffer trouble, as a criminal, even unto bonds
Heb. 13:3 – remember them that are in bonds, as bound with them

**7. Chasten**

Early Christians are described as victims of violent chastening and encouraged to accept it as discipline resulting in peaceable fruits of righteousness. For their part, Christians must seek peace with everyone.

II Cor. 6:9 - As unknown, and yet well known; as dying, and, behold, we live; as chastened, and not killed
Heb. 12:3-14 - Consider him who endured from sinners such hostility against himself, so that you may not grow weary or fainthearted. In your struggle against sin you have not yet resisted to the point of shedding your blood. And have you forgotten the exhortation which addresses you as sons? --"My son, do not regard lightly the discipline of the Lord, nor lose courage when you are chastened by him. For the Lord disciplines him whom he loves, and chastises every son whom he receives." It is for discipline that you have to endure. God is treating you as sons; for what son is there whom his father does not discipline? If you are

left without discipline, in which all have participated, then you are illegitimate children and not sons. Besides this, we have had earthly fathers to discipline us and we respected them. Shall we not much more be subject to the Father of spirits and live? For they disciplined us for a short time at their pleasure, but he disciplines us for our good, that we may share his holiness. For the moment all discipline seems painful rather than pleasant; later it yields the peaceful fruit of righteousness to those who have been trained by it. Strive for peace with all men, and for the holiness without which no one will see the Lord.

## 8. Compassion

Compassion and empathy for others are characteristic of the way of God's chosen ones.

Col. 3:12 – Put on then, as God's chosen ones, holy and beloved, compassion
I Pet. 3:8 – having compassion one for another; be pitiful

## 9. Court of Law

Followers of Jesus are described as victims of legal action and are discouraged from going to court against anyone. It is better to be treated unjustly than to go to court.

Matt. 5:40 – if any one sues you in a court of law, and takes away your coat, let him have your shirt as well

I Cor. 6:1-10 – now therefore there is utterly a fault among you, because you go to a court of law against each other. Why don't you rather allow yourselves to be treated unjustly?
James 2:6 – do not rich people oppress you, and bring you before courts of law?

## 10. Death

Christians did not fear death, were persecuted to death, and never sought the death of others. In their manner of dying, God's people demonstrate the way of life resulting from the message about Jesus.

Acts 21:13 – I am ready not only to be bound, but also to die at Jerusalem for the name of the Lord
Acts 22:4 – I persecuted this Way unto the death
I Cor. 15:54-56 – Death is swallowed up in victory. O death, where is your sting? O grave, where is your victory?
II Cor. 4:11 – we who are alive are always delivered to death for Jesus' sake, that the life also of Jesus might be clearly seen in our perishable body
Phil. 1:21 – for to me to live is Christ and to die is gain

## 11. Destroy

Disciples need not fear those who inflict physical death but only eternal consequences.

Matt. 10:28 – fear not those who kill the body, but are not able to kill the soul, but rather fear him who is able to destroy both body and soul in hell

**12. Do Good**

Doing good to one's enemies is the only option and is how one becomes a child of God. Doing evil or harm to others is not the way of the disciple, for doing good must be the response to physical attack or verbal abuse from others.

Lk. 6:27,28 – do good to them that hate you
Lk. 6:33 – if you do good to them that do good to you, what credit is that to you?
Lk. 6:35 - do good (to enemies) …and you will be sons of the Most High; for he is kind to the ungrateful and the selfish.
Gal. 5:22 - the fruit of the Spirit is …goodness
Gal. 6:10 – do good unto all men
Eph. 6:8 – whatever good thing anyone does, the same he will receive from the Lord
Rom. 12:21 – overcome evil with good
Heb. 13:16 – forget not to do good
III Jn.11 – he who does good is of God

**13. Endurance**

The patient endurance of unjust suffering is the hallmark of Christian conduct and the only response in the face of persecution or any injustice.

II Tim. 2:3 – You therefore endure hardness as a good soldier of Jesus Christ
II Tim. 3:11 – what persecutions I endured
II Thess. 1:4 – we glory in you for your patience in all your persecutions and tribulations that you endure
Heb. 10:32 – you endured a great fight of afflictions
Heb. 12:3,7 – consider Him who endured.... If you endure discipline, God is treating you as his children
James 5:11 – behold, we count them happy who endure
I Peter 2:19 – for this is commendable, if a person for conscience toward God endures pain, suffering wrongfully

**14. Enemy**

Enemies must be addressed only with love and goodness as the way to imitate God who loved us when we were his enemies and who blesses everyone.

Matt. 5:44 - But I say unto you, Love your enemies, bless them that curse you, do good to them that hate you, and pray for them which despitefully use you, and persecute you
Luke 6:27 - But I say unto you which hear, Love your enemies, do good to them which hate you
Luke 6:35 - But love your enemies, and do good, and lend, hoping for nothing again; and your reward shall be great, and you shall be

the children of the Highest: for he is kind to the unthankful and to the evil

Rom. 5:10 - For if, when we were enemies, we were reconciled to God by the death of his Son, much more, being reconciled, we shall be saved by his life

Rom. 12:20 - Therefore if your enemy is hungry, feed him; if he is thirsty, give him drink: for in so doing you shall heap coals of fire on his head.

## 15. Evil

Christians suffer evil but are admonished repeatedly to never pay back evil with evil but only respond with doing good to enemies.

Acts 9:13 – how much evil he has done to your saints at Jerusalem

Rom. 3:8 – Shall we do evil that good may come?

Rom. 12:21 – Be not overcome by evil, but overcome evil with good.

Rom. 12:17 – Do not pay back anyone evil for evil.

I Thess. 5:15 – see that no one renders evil for evil toward anyone... but always do good to everyone

I Peter 3:9 – not rendering evil for evil

## 16. Fight

Citizens of the divine kingdom do not engage in physical fighting.

John 18:36 - Jesus answered, My kingdom is not of this world: if my kingdom were of this world, then would my servants fight, that I should not be delivered to the Jews: but now is my kingdom not from here.

### 17. Force
Jesus, his followers, and his kingdom are victims of others who use physical force.

Matt. 5:41 – and whoever shall force you to go one mile, go with him two
Matt. 11:12 – the kingdom of heaven suffers violence, and the violent take it by force
John 6:15 – when Jesus therefore understood that they wanted to come and take him by force, to make him a king, he left
Acts 23:10 – the chief captain… commanded the soldiers to go down, and to take him from them by force

### 18. Forgiveness
A quarrel or offense should always be approached with a readiness to forgive because God forgave us in Christ's death. Our being forgiven by God depends upon our forgiving others.

Matt. 6:14 - For if you forgive people their trespasses, your heavenly Father will also forgive you.

Matt. 6:15 - But if you forgive not men their trespasses, neither will your Father forgive your trespasses.
Luke 6:37 - Judge not, and you shall not be judged: condemn not, and you shall not be condemned: forgive, and you shall be forgiven
Eph. 4:32 - And be kind one to another, tenderhearted, forgiving one another, even as God for Christ's sake has forgiven you.
Col. 3:13 - Forbearing one another, and forgiving one another, if any man have a quarrel against any: even as Christ forgave you, so also do you.

**19. Gentleness**

Gentleness is the opposite of physical fighting, is a sign of being led by the Spirit, is a result of divine wisdom, and must be shown to everyone.

Gal. 5:22 – the fruit of the Spirit is… gentleness
II Tim.2:24 – be gentle to all men
Titus 3:2 – to speak evil of no man, to be no brawlers, but gentle
James 3:17 - the wisdom that is from above is first pure, then peaceable, gentle, and easy to be intreated, full of mercy

**20. Harmless/Harm**

Doing good can prevent harm done to you, and God's people must be harmless, as their Lord, to set themselves apart from the world.

Matt. 10:16 – be therefore... harmless as doves
Philippians 2:15 - That you may be blameless and harmless, the sons of God, without rebuke, in the midst of a crooked and perverse nation, among whom you shine as lights in the world
Heb. 7:26 - For such an high priest became us, who is holy, harmless, undefiled, separate from sinners, and made higher than the heavens
1 Peter 3:13 - And who is he that will harm you, if you are followers of that which is good?

**21. Hate**

Christians may be hated but they must never hate others and must do good to those who hate them. Being hated for Jesus, is a blessed state because Jesus was also hated. One cannot hate another person and also love God.

Matt. 5:43 - You have heard that it was said, You shall love your neighbour, and hate your enemy.
Matt. 5:44 - But I say to you, Love your enemies, bless those who curse you, do good to those hate you, and pray for those who despitefully use you, and persecute you
Matt. 10:22 - And you shall be hated by all men for my name's sake: but he who endures to the end shall be saved.
Matt. 24:9 - Then shall they deliver you up to be afflicted, and shall kill you: and you shall be hated by all nations for my name's sake.

Luke 1:71 - That we should be saved from our enemies, and from the hand of all that hate us.

Luke 6:22 - Blessed are you, when men shall hate you, and when they shall separate you from their company, and shall reproach you, and cast out your name as evil, for the Son of man's sake.

Luke 6:27 - But I say to you who hear, Love your enemies, do good to those who hate you.

Luke 21:17 - And you shall be hated by all men for my name's sake.

John 15:18 - If the world hate you, you know that it hated me before it hated you.

John 15:19 - If you were of the world, the world would love its own: but because you are not of the world, but I have chosen you out of the world, therefore the world hates you.

John 17:14 - I have given them your word; and the world has hated them, because they are not of the world, even as I am not of the world.

I John 2:9 - He who said he is in the light, and hates his brother, is in darkness even until now.

I John 2:11 - But he who hates his brother is in darkness, and walks in darkness, and knows not where he goes, because darkness has blinded his eyes.

I John 3:13 – Do not be surprised, my brethren, if the world hates you.

I John 3:15 - Whoever hates his brother is a murderer: and you know that no murderer has eternal life abiding in him.

I John 4:20 - If a man says, I love God, and hates his brother, he is a liar: for he who loves not his brother whom he has seen, how can he love God whom he has not seen?

## 22. Honor

The implications are far-reaching, for if there are no exceptions, this means Christians must honor their enemies, drunks, and those who do not honor themselves.

Rom. 12:10 – in honor preferring one another
I Pet. 2:17 – honor all men

## 23. Humility

Humility is an attitude that God approves most highly. This means to treat others with such dignity and respect that the person you are with becomes the most valued and important person.

Matt. 23:12 – he who humbles himself shall be exalted
Lk. 14:11 – he who humbles himself shall be exalted
Acts 20:19 – serving the Lord with all humility of mind
Col.3:12 – put on humility
James 4:6 – God resists the proud, but gives grace unto the humble
I Peter 5:5 – be clothed with humility: for God resists the proud, and gives grace to the humble

## 24. Kill

While the law of Moses prohibits murder, still Christians were killed as was Jesus. Those who kill us should not be feared. James says although the saints of God are killed, they do not rise up or engage in violent resistance. In scripture, Christians are always victims of killing but never kill others in self-defense or otherwise.

Matt. 5:21 - You have heard that it was said by them of old time, You shall not kill; and whosoever shall kill shall be in danger of the judgment

Matt. 10:28 - And fear not those who kill the body, but are not able to kill the soul

Matt. 16:21 - From that time on began Jesus to show to his disciples, how that he must go unto Jerusalem, and suffer many things by the elders and chief priests and scribes, and be killed

Matt. 23:34 - I send to you prophets, and wise men, and scribes: and some of them you shall kill and crucify; and some of them shall you scourge in your synagogues, and persecute them from city to city

Matt. 24:9 - Then shall they deliver you up to be afflicted, and shall kill you: and you shall be hated by all nations for my name's sake.

Luke 12:4 - And I say to you my friends, Be not afraid of those who kill the body, and after that have no more that they can do.

Acts 9:23 - And after many days had passed, the Jews took counsel to kill him:
Acts 9:24 - But their lying in wait was known by Saul. And they watched the gates day and night to kill him.
Acts 12:2 - And he killed James the brother of John with the sword.
Acts 23:12 - And when it was day, certain of the Jews banded together, and bound themselves under a curse, saying that they would neither eat nor drink till they had killed Paul.
Acts 26:21 - For these reasons the Jews caught me in the temple, and went about to kill me.
Rom. 8:36 - As it is written, For your sake we are killed all the day long; we are accounted as sheep for the slaughter.
James 5:6 - You have condemned and killed the just; and he does not resist you.

## 25. Kindness

The grace of God is undeserved kindness toward us. When we show kindness to violent people, we are imitating God, and so it is a sign of our calling as servants of God and a result of the Spirit in their lives.

Luke 6:35 – love your enemies, do good, and lend hoping for nothing again… and you shall be sons of the Most High: for he is kind to the unthankful and to the evil
I Cor. 13:4 – love is kind

II Cor. 6:6 – approving ourselves as ministers of God by kindness
Gal. 5:22 – the fruit of the Spirit is… kindness
Eph. 4:32 – and be kind one to another
Col. 3:12 – put on kindness
II Peter 1:7 – add to brotherly kindness, love

**26. Longsuffering**

God's people must put on longsuffering, sometimes translated as patience or perseverance, and it is to be exercised in the face of hostile opposition. It is a sign one is led by the Spirit and that one is approved as a servant of God. Notice that joyfulness should accompany this virtue.

II Cor. 6:6 – approving ourselves as ministers of God by longsuffering
Gal. 5:22 – the fruit of the Spirit is… longsuffering
Eph. 4:2 – walk worthy of the vocation to which you were called, with longsuffering
Col. 1:11 – strengthened with all might unto longsuffering with joyfulness
Col. 3:12 – put on as God's elect, longsuffering
II Tim. 3:10 – you have fully known my longsuffering

**27. Love**

The kind of love in the following passages is undeserved or unconditional kindness. This is the love God had for the world in giving Jesus to be a sacrifice for sin. This love prefers to die rather than to kill because it is sacrificial in imitation of the love of Jesus in taking on the sins of the world in his suffering and death.

Matt. 5:44,46 – love your enemies….no reward in loving those who love you
Matt. 19:19; 22:39 – love your neighbor as yourself
Lk. 6:27-32 – love, bless, do good, pray for enemies
Jn. 13:34 – love one another
Jn. 15:12,17 – love one another
Jn. 15:13 – greater love has no man than to lay down his life
Rom. 12:9 – let love be genuine
Rom. 13:8 – owe no one anything but to love
Rom. 13:10 - Love does no wrong to a neighbor; therefore love is the fulfilling of the law.
I Cor. 13:4-7 – love is patient and kind,… is not irritable or resentful… bears all things,… endures all things
I Cor. 16:14 – let all things be done in love
Gal. 5:13 – by love serve one another
Gal. 5:22 – love is fruit of the Spirit
Eph. 4:2 – bearing with one another in love
Eph. 5:2 – walk in love
I Pet. 2:17 – love the brotherhood
I Jn. 2:15 – love not things in the world
I Jn. 3:16,17 – love is to give to the needs of others and to lay down one's life
I Jn. 4:10 – love others because God loves them

**28. Lowliness**

The nature of Jesus is to be lowly in heart, and this is what he wants his people to be also. Lowliness does not allow physical aggression against anyone because it is linked to meekness, forbearance, patience, and love.

Matt. 11:29 - Take my yoke upon you, and learn of me, for I am meek and lowly in heart
Eph. 4:2 - With all lowliness and meekness, with longsuffering, forbearing one another in love
Phil. 2:3 – in lowliness of mind let each esteem others better than themselves

**29. Meekness**

The definition of meekness is gentleness in the face of wrath, patient and unresentful under injury and reproach, and this understanding of meek complements the other values of mercifulness and peacemaking found among the beatitudes (Mat. 5: 5,7,9). Meekness is a sign of the indwelling Spirit and must be shown to all people.

Matt. 5:5 – blessed are the meek
Gal. 5:23 – the fruit of the Spirit is… meekness
Col. 3:12 – put on meekness
I Tim. 6:11 – follow after meekness
Titus 3:2 – show all meekness to all men
I Peter 3:15 – be ready to give an answer… with meekness

## 30. Mercy

God is merciful to enemies, and in imitation of God his people must shown mercy to their enemies. Full mercy toward enemies is the wisdom that comes only from God.

Matt. 5:7 – blessed are the merciful
Lk. 6:36 – be therefore merciful, as your Father also is merciful
James 2:13 – he shall have judgment without mercy, who has shown no mercy
James 3:17 – the wisdom that is from above is... full of mercy

## 31. Overcome

Regardless of the kind of tribulation, Christians can remain happy in knowing that Jesus has overcome. To overcome or defeat evil, one should use acts of goodness toward one's enemy. Spiritual weapons, especially our faith, are strong enough to overcome any evil the world may do to us.

John 16:33 - I have said this to you, that in me you may have peace. In the world you have tribulation; but be of good cheer, I have overcome the world.
Rom. 12:21 - Do not be overcome by evil, but overcome evil with good.
I John 4:4 - Little children, you are of God, and have overcome them; for he who is in you is greater than he who is in the world.

I John 5:4 - For whatever is born of God overcomes the world; and this is the victory that overcomes the world, our faith.

## 32. Patience

Servants of God are approved by their patience as a glorious response to be exercised toward all men and in all kinds of trouble including unjust physical suffering inflicted by enemies and not only in persecution.

Rom. 5:3,4 – tribulation produces patience (endurance)
II Cor. 6:4 – approving ourselves as ministers of God in much patience
I Tim. 6:11 – O man of God, follow after patience
I Thess. 5:14 - Now we exhort you, brethren... be patient toward all men.
II Tim. 2:24 – the servant of the Lord must be patient
II Thess. 1:4 – we glory in you for your patience in all your persecutions and tribulations that you endure
James 5:7,8,10 – take, my brethren, the prophets for an example of suffering affliction, and of patience. Behold we count them happy which endure
I Pet. 2:20 – if, when you do right and suffer for it, you take it patiently, you have God's approval. For even hereunto were you called...

## 33. Peace

Children of God are peacemakers who bring a gospel of peace given by the Prince of Peace. This peace is not only in the message of forgiveness but is also demonstrated in the conduct of Christians toward their enemies. This peaceful conduct is linked to the character of gentleness, mercy, and being open to reason. Following peace with everyone is a condition of eternal salvation.

Matt. 5:9 - Blessed are the peacemakers: for they shall be called the children of God.
Mark 9:50 - Salt is good: but if the salt has lost its saltiness, how then will you season it? Have salt in yourselves, and have peace one with another.
Luke 1:79 - To give light to them that sit in darkness and in the shadow of death, to guide our feet into the way of peace.
Luke 2:14 - Glory to God in the highest, and on earth peace, good will toward men.
John 14:27 - Peace I leave with you, my peace I give unto you: not as the world gives, give I unto you. Let not your heart be troubled, neither let it be afraid.
Acts 10:36 - The word which God sent unto the children of Israel, preaching peace by Jesus Christ
Rom. 3:17 - And the way of peace have they not known
Rom. 10:15 - And how shall they preach, except they be sent? as it is written, How beautiful are

the feet of them that preach the gospel of peace, and bring glad tidings of good things!

Rom. 12:18 - If it be possible, as much as lies in you, live peaceably with all men.

Rom. 14:19 - Let us therefore follow after the things which make for peace, and things wherewith one may edify another.

Rom. 15:33 - Now the God of peace be with you all.

II Cor. 13:11 - Finally, brethren, farewell. Be perfect, be of good comfort, be of one mind, live in peace; and the God of love and peace shall be with you.

Gal. 5:22 - But the fruit of the Spirit is… peace

Eph. 6:15 - And your feet shod with the preparation of the gospel of peace

I Thess. 5:13 - And be at peace among yourselves.

II Thess. 3:16 - Now the Lord of peace himself give you peace always by all means.

I Tim. 2:2 - For kings, and for all that are in authority; that we may lead a quiet and peaceable life in all godliness and honesty.

Heb. 7:2 - first being by interpretation King of righteousness, and after that also King of Salem, which is, King of peace

Heb. 12:14 - Follow peace with all men, and holiness, without which no man shall see the Lord.

James 3:17 - But the wisdom from above is first pure, then peaceable, gentle, open to reason, full of mercy

James 3:18 - And the harvest of righteousness is sown in peace by those who make peace.
I Peter 3:11 - let him turn away from evil and do right; let him seek peace and pursue it.

## 34. Persecution

Persecution is any unjust attack both verbal and physical. Christians may flee but may not use physical means to defend themselves. They are always in scripture the victims of persecution and not perpetrators, as it is written, he who was born after the flesh persecuted him who was born after the Spirit. Christians should take pleasure in suffering persecution.

Matt. 5:10 - Blessed are they who are persecuted for righteousness' sake: for theirs is the kingdom of heaven.
Matt. 5:11 - Blessed are ye, when men shall revile you, and persecute you
Matt. 5:12 - so persecuted they the prophets who were before you.
Matt. 5:44 - pray for those who despitefully use you, and persecute you
Matt. 10:23 - But when they persecute you in this city, flee into another
Matt. 13:21 - when tribulation or persecution arises because of the word, eventually he is offended.
Matt. 23:34 - I send unto you prophets, and wise men, and scribes: and some of them you shall kill and crucify; and some of them shall

you scourge in your synagogues, and persecute them from city to city.

Luke 21:12 - But before all these, they shall lay their hands on you, and persecute you

John 15:20 - Remember the word that I said to you, The servant is not greater than his master. If they have persecuted me, they will also persecute you

Acts 8:1 - at that time there was a great persecution against the church that was at Jerusalem

Acts 13:50 - raised persecution against Paul and Barnabas, and expelled them out of their coasts.

Acts 22:4 - And I persecuted this way unto the death, binding and delivering into prisons both men and women.

Rom. 8:35 - Who shall separate us from the love of Christ? shall ... persecution... or sword?

Rom. 12:14 - Bless those who persecute you: bless, and curse not.

I Cor. 4:12 - being persecuted, we suffer it.

I Cor. 15:9 - I persecuted the church of God.

II Cor. 4:9 - Persecuted, but not forsaken; cast down, but not destroyed.

II Cor. 12:10 - Therefore I take pleasure ... in reproaches... in persecutions

Gal. 1:13 - in the Jews' religion, how that beyond measure I persecuted the church of God, and wasted it.

Gal. 4:29 - But as then, he who was born after the flesh persecuted him who was born after the Spirit, even so it is now.

Gal. 6:12 - suffer persecution for the cross of Christ.

Phil. 3:6 - Concerning zeal, persecuting the church

I Thess. 2:15 - Who both killed the Lord Jesus, and their own prophets, and have persecuted us

II Thess. 1:4 - So that we ourselves glory in you in the churches of God for your patience and faith in all your persecutions and tribulations that you endure.

I Tim. 1:13 - Who was before a blasphemer, and a persecutor, and injurious: but I obtained mercy, because I did it ignorantly in unbelief.

II Tim. 3:11 - Persecutions, afflictions, that came to me at Antioch, at Iconium, at Lystra; what persecutions I endured

II Tim. 3:12 - all that will live godly in Christ Jesus shall suffer persecution.

Rev. 12:13 - And when the dragon saw that he was cast unto the earth, he persecuted the woman which brought forth the man child.

### 35. Plunder

Christians were victims of plundering and did not retaliate but suffered joyfully.

Heb. 10:34 – you joyfully accepted the plundering of your property

## 36. Recompense/Repay/Pay back

Only God can punish or pay back evil for evil done to Christians who can never use physical force or the threat of physical force to right the wrongs done to them.

Rom. 12:17 – recompense to no one evil for evil
II Thess. 1:6 – it is a righteous thing with God to recompense tribulation to them that trouble you
Heb. 10:30 – vengeance belongs to me, I will recompense, says the Lord

## 37. Reproach

The definition of reproach is verbal abuse that causes shame or disgrace such as cursing, demeaning sarcasm and name-calling. Jesus and his followers are victims of this kind of attack, and can cope by taking pleasure when reproached for doing what is right. The proper response is to love, bless, and pray for the abuser.

Luke 6:22 - Blessed are you, when men shall hate you… and shall reproach you, and cast out your name as evil, for the Son of man's sake.
Rom. 15:3 - For even Christ pleased not himself; but, as it is written, The reproaches of those who reproached you fell on me.
II Cor. 12:10 - Therefore I take pleasure in infirmities, in reproaches… for Christ's sake: for when I am weak, then am I strong.

I Tim. 4:10 - For therefore we both labour and suffer reproach, because we trust in the living God

Heb. 10:33 - Partly, while you were made a spectacle both by reproaches and afflictions; and partly, while you became companions of them that were so used.

Heb. 11:26 - Esteeming the reproach of Christ greater riches than the treasures in Egypt

Heb. 13:13 - Let us go forth therefore unto him without the camp, bearing his reproach.

I Peter 4:14 - If you are reproached for the name of Christ, happy are you

## 38. Resist

The term resist means to remain firm against or oppose. In the face of a physical insult such as a slap, Christians are taught to accept it without retaliation. But the whole of scripture shows this non-resistance may lead to the death of the one who does God's will. The Hebrew passage speaks of Christians refusing to give in to sin leading to their own death, not the death of their enemy.

Matt. 5:39 - But I say to you, That you resist not the evil one: but whoever shall strike you on your cheek, turn to him the other also.

Heb. 12:4 - You have not yet resisted until shedding your own blood, striving against sin.

James 5:6 - You have condemned and killed the just; and he does not resist you.

## 39. Revile

To revile means to assail with abusive language. The unrepentant reviler cannot be saved. Christians bless rather than revile in return and are happy when reviled for doing right.

Matt. 5:11 - Blessed are you, when men shall revile you... for my sake.
Matt. 27:39 - And they who passed by reviled him, wagging their heads,
Mark 15:32 - And they that were crucified with him reviled him.
I Cor. 4:12 - being reviled, we bless
I Cor. 6:10 - nor revilers... shall inherit the kingdom of God.
I Peter 2:23 - Who, when he was reviled, reviled not again

## 40. Smite

Christians should turn the other cheek when struck in the face. To strike back at the enemy is not an option for the Christian.

Matt. 5:39 - But I say to you, That you resist not evil: but whoever shall smite you on your right cheek, turn to him the other also.
Luke 22:63 - And the men that held Jesus mocked him, and smote him.
John 18:23 - Jesus answered him, If I have spoken evil, bear witness of the evil: but if well, why do you smite me?

Acts 23:2 - And the high priest Ananias commanded those who stood by him to smite him on the mouth.
II Cor. 11:20 - For you bear it if a man... strikes you in the face.

**41. Stoned**

The law of Moses called for those violators to be stoned to death. In contrast, the law of Christ called for Christians to do good to their enemies and not to seek their punishment but to allow God to avenge any wrong. Christians were only victims of stoning and were never perpetrators.

Acts 7:58 - And cast him out of the city, and stoned him: and the witnesses laid down their clothes at a young man's feet, whose name was Saul.
Acts 7:59 - And they stoned Stephen, calling upon God, and saying, Lord Jesus, receive my spirit.
Acts 14:5 - And when there was an assault made both by the Gentiles, and also by the Jews with their rulers, to use them despitefully, and to stone them,
Acts 14:19 - And there came there certain Jews from Antioch and Iconium, who persuaded the people, and having stoned Paul, drew him out of the city, supposing he had been dead.
II Cor. 11:25 – Three times was I beaten with rods, once was I stoned

Heb. 11:37 - They were stoned, they were sawn apart, were tempted, were slain with the sword

## 42. Strike

Notice that the quality of a bishop is not only to be no striker but also not easily angered. Peter was told to put away his sword rather than to employ it in striking others.

Matt. 26:51,52 - And, behold, one of them who was with Jesus stretched out his hand, and drew his sword, and struck a servant of the high priest's, and smote off his ear. Then said Jesus to him, Put up again your sword into its place: for all those who take the sword shall perish with the sword.
Mark 14:65 - And some began to spit on him, and to cover his face, and to beat him…and the servants did strike him with the palms of their hands.
I Tim. 3:3 - Not given to wine, no striker…but patient, not a brawler
Titus 1:7 - For a bishop must be … not soon angry… no striker

## 43. Stripes

Jesus and his followers received stripes or flogging but never inflicted it on others.

Acts 16:23 - And when they had laid many stripes upon them, they cast them into prison, charging the jailor to keep them safely

II Cor. 6:5 - In stripes, in imprisonments, in tumults, in labours, in watchings, in fastings
II Cor. 11:23 - Are they ministers of Christ? (I speak as a fool) I am more; in labours more abundant, in stripes above measure, in prisons more frequent, in deaths oft.
II Cor. 11:24 - By the Jews five times received I forty stripes less one.
II Peter 2:24 - Who himself bore our sins in his own body on the tree, that we, being dead to sins, should live unto righteousness: by whose stripes you were healed.

## 44. Suffering

Suffering for doing what is right is the joyful state of Christians. Knowing about the suffering of other Christians and of Jesus, gives us courage to face the same. Suffering for doing what is right, must be taken patiently without hatred or resentment. We are called to follow the example of Jesus in his patient way of suffering injustice. Those of the kingdom of heaven are victims of violence but never use violence against others.

Matt. 11:12 – the kingdom of heaven suffers violence and the violent take it by force
Matt. 17:12 – likewise shall also the son of man suffer
Acts 5:41 – rejoicing that they were counted worthy to suffer shame for his name

Rom. 8:17 – heirs of God, and joint-heirs with Christ, if so be that we suffer with him, that we may be also glorified together

Rom. 8:18 – the sufferings of this present time are not worthy to be compared with the glory that shall be revealed in us

I Cor. 4:12 – being persecuted, we suffer it

II Cor. 1:5 – the sufferings of Christ abound in us

II Cor. 1:6 – whether we be afflicted, it is for your consolation and salvation, which is effectual in the enduring of the same sufferings which we also suffer

II Cor. 1:7 – you are partakers of the sufferings

Gal. 3:4 – have you suffered so many things in vain?

Gal. 6:12 – lest they should suffer persecution for the cross of Christ

Phil. 1:29 – to you it is given on behalf of Christ, not only to believe on him, but also to suffer for his sake

Phil. 3:10 – that I may know the fellowship of his sufferings, being made conformable to his death

Col. 1:24 – who now rejoice in my sufferings for you

I Thess. 2:2 – we had suffered before, and were shamefully treated as you know

I Thess. 2:14 – for you have also suffered similar things by your own countrymen

II Thess. 1:5 – your patience and faith in all your persecutions that you endure that you may be counted worthy of the kingdom of God, for which you also suffer

II Tim. 1:12 – because of which I also suffer these things

II Tim. 2:9,12 – if we suffer we shall also reign with him

II Tim. 3:12 – everyone who lives godly in Christ Jesus shall suffer persecution

I Peter 2:19 - For one is approved if, mindful of God, he endures pain while suffering unjustly.

I Peter 2:20 - But if when you do right and suffer for it you take it patiently, you have God's approval.

I Peter 2:21 - For to this you have been called, because Christ also suffered for you, leaving you an example, that you should follow in his steps.

I Peter 2:23 - When he was reviled, he did not revile in return; when he suffered, he did not threaten; but he trusted to him who judges justly.

I Peter 3:14 - But even if you do suffer for righteousness' sake, you will be blessed.

I Peter 3:17 - For it is better to suffer for doing right, if that should be God's will, than for doing wrong.

I Peter 3:18 - For Christ also suffered for sins once for all, the righteous for the unrighteous

I Peter 4:1 - Since therefore Christ suffered in the flesh, arm yourselves with the same thought, for whoever has suffered in the flesh has ceased from sin

I Peter 4:13 – But rejoice in so far as you share Christ's sufferings, that you may also rejoice and be glad when his glory is revealed.

I Peter 4:16 - yet if one suffers as a Christian, let him not be ashamed, but under that name let him glorify God.

I Peter 4:19 - Therefore let those who suffer according to God's will do right and entrust their souls to a faithful Creator.

I Peter 5:10 - And after you have suffered a little while, the God of all grace, who has called you to his eternal glory in Christ, will himself restore, establish, and strengthen you.

Rev. 2:10 – fear none of those things that you shall suffer

**45. Threaten**

In scripture the enemies of God's people threatened physical harm to them. In suffering unjust physical attack, Christians must follow Jesus' example in not threatening their enemies. When Christian masters were instructed not to threaten their slaves, this included threats of physical harm and in effect implied that slaves could leave without being forced to return.

Acts 4:17 - But that it spread no further among the people, let us strongly threaten them, that they speak to no one in this name from now on.

Acts 4:21 - So when they had further threatened them, they let them go, finding nothing how they might punish them

Acts 4:29 - And now, Lord, see their threatenings: and grant to your servants, that with all boldness they may speak your word

Acts 9:1 - And Saul, still shouting threatenings and slaughter against the disciples of the Lord, went to the high priest

Eph. 6:9 - And masters, do the same things unto them, do not threaten: knowing that your Master also is in heaven; neither is there respect of persons with him.

I Peter 2:23 - Who, when he was reviled, reviled not again; when he suffered, he threatened not; but committed himself to him who judges righteously

## 46. Tribulation

The word tribulation in these passages refers to difficulties and persecutions of every kind caused by those who oppose our faith. Christians can "glory" in this when they suffer patiently. Comfort in tribulation comes from God.

John 16:33 - These things I have spoken to you, that in me you might have peace. In the world you shall have tribulation: but be of good cheer; I have overcome the world.

Acts 14:22 - we must through much tribulation enter into the kingdom of God.

Rom. 5:3 - And not only so, but we glory in tribulations also: knowing that tribulation works patience

Rom. 8:35 - Who shall separate us from the love of Christ? shall tribulation... or persecution... or sword?

Rom. 12:12 - patient in tribulation

II Cor. 1:4 - Who comforts us in all our tribulation, that we may be able to comfort them which are in any trouble, by the comfort wherewith we ourselves are comforted by God.

II Cor. 7:4 - Great is my boldness of speech toward you, great is my glorying in you: I am filled with comfort, I am exceeding joyful in all our tribulation.

Eph. 3:13 - Wherefore I desire that you faint not at my tribulations for you which is your glory.

I Thess. 3:4 - For truly, when we were with you, we told you before that we should suffer tribulation

II Thess. 1:4 - So that we ourselves glory in you in the churches of God for your patience and faith in all your persecutions and tribulations that you endure.

Rev. 1:9 - I John, who also am your brother, and companion in tribulation

Rev. 2:10 - Fear none of those things which you shall suffer: behold, the devil shall cast some of you into prison, that you may be tried; and you shall have tribulation ten days: be faithful unto death, and I will give you a crown of life.

**47. Terror**
Christians should not be afraid of the terrible threats and trouble caused by the physical attacks and verbal abuse of others.

I Peter 3:14 – be not afraid of their terror, neither be troubled

**48. Vengeance**
Christians can firmly rely upon the judgment of God against their enemies and must never exercise vengeance of any kind against them.

Luke 18:7-8 - And shall not God avenge his own elect, who cry day and night to him, though he bear long with them? I tell you that he will avenge them speedily.
Rom. 12:19 - Dearly beloved, avenge not yourselves, but rather wait for divine wrath: for it is written, Vengeance is mine; I will repay, says the Lord. Therefore if your enemy is hungry, feed him; if he is thirsty, give him drink
1 Thess. 4:6 - That no man go beyond and defraud his brother in any matter: because the Lord is the avenger of all such, as we also have warned you before and testified.
Heb. 10:30 - For we know him who has said, Vengeance belongs unto me, I will repay, says

the Lord. And again, The Lord shall judge his people.

Rev. 6:10 - And they cried with a loud voice, saying, How long, O Lord, holy and true, do you not judge and avenge our blood on them that dwell on the earth?

Rev. 18:20 - Rejoice over her, you heaven, and you holy apostles and prophets; for God has avenged you on her.

Rev. 19:2 - For true and righteous are his judgments: for he has judged the great whore, who corrupted the earth with her fornication, and has avenged the blood of his servants at her hand.

**49. Violence**

Physical violence is done to the kingdom of heaven. John the Baptist disarmed soldiers by telling them to do no violence to anyone. This is the rule of the kingdom of God in contrast to the rule given to Israel by Moses.

Matt. 11:12 - And from the days of John the Baptist until now the kingdom of heaven suffers violence, and the violent take it by force.

Luke 3:14 - And the soldiers likewise demanded him, saying, And what shall we do? And he said to them, Do violence to no one, neither accuse any falsely; and be content with your wages.

Acts 21:35 - And when he came upon the stairs, so it was, that he was carried by the soldiers because of the violence of the people.

## 50. War/Warfare/Weapons

Paul states the case of pacifism and non-violence very clearly in this passage in which Christians are reminded that although they live in the physical world, their warfare and their weapons are not physical yet have great power in the war between good and evil.

II Cor. 10:3-5 - For though we live in the physical, we do not engage in physical warfare For the weapons of our warfare are not physical, but mighty through God to the pulling down of strong holds; casting down imaginations, and every high thing that exalts itself against the knowledge of God, and bringing into captivity every thought to the obedience of Christ

*Part III*

*Radical Applications*

*Introduction*

Perhaps too often in the corporate life of the Christian community and in the lives of individual disciples, there is an absence of the real application of the teaching of Jesus who gave warning concerning the foolish and wise builders: the foolish who hear the word of God but do not put it into practice and the wise who do the word of God. James also spoke of one who looks into the perfect law of liberty as into a mirror but then turns away forgetting what he looks like (James 1:22-24).

The ideas presented here are an effort to provide examples of how the radical teachings of Jesus can be put into practice. These projects should be done in Jesus' name so that God can be glorified. However, caution is to be exercised by observing that a "project" cannot substitute for the sacrificial way of life as the disciple "takes up his cross daily" (Luke 9:23).

*Applications For Radical Christianity*

Often radical biblical Christianity is confused with popular ideas about Christianity. **Hold a conference** or public discussion entitled "Early Christianity versus Popular Christianity."

Living out the radical teachings of Jesus is difficult and requires courage that is most successful when supported by a group of committed radical disciples. Start a **"Radical Christian Support Group."**

Letting your light shine can mean going public with the teachings of Jesus. When your church or group decides to embark on a radical project, distribute a **press release** and hold a press conference. Be prepared for opposition and persecution from within your church and from the community.

Join others in your church to start a **"Radical Christian Community"** or Commune where the theme or purpose is to support each other as you live out the peace and justice teachings of the New Testament by living simply and in promoting different radical projects. Give money saved, to poor Christians and churches in famine areas.

## *Applications For Radical Peace Politics*

Organize a **"Mediation and Conflict Resolution Service"** as an alternative for people who would otherwise seek a remedy through the courts.

Often the most important social issues are avoided or addressed only through the biased media. Host the **"Institute for Mutual Understanding"** in your city, that has the purpose of inviting speakers with differing views on a hot topic such as causes of homosexuality, intelligent design and evolution, fundamentalist and secular Islam, atheism and theism, and other topics as they emerge in your region or country.

Learning practical **skills for managing conflict**, hostility, and name-calling, can be a valuable experience. Hold a training workshop on conflict resolution, in which you teach and demonstrate empathic reflective listening with practice exercises for those attending. Use the chapter on "How To Manage Conflict" as a handout.

Invite a well-known representative of a hostile group, e.g. fundamentalist Muslims, to your city and **demonstrate empathic reflective listening** as the guest elaborates on his points of view that many find offensive.

The actual practice of non-resistance in specific situations is challenging. Hold a **special class to play out scenarios** when circumstances are beyond one's control and when one is a victim of unjust physical violence.

Invite people to a workshop on **"Making a Defense in Court."** Include addressing the judge respectfully, making objections, cross-examination, questioning your witnesses, presenting evidence in an organized manner, preparing written submissions, and providing an effective closing statement.

A way to disarm a potential enemy is to make friends with them. Organize a **"Muslim Outreach Team"** and begin making friends with Moslems in your community. Invite them to dinner and make them part of your activities. Let them know that Jesus taught to love your enemies and that he died on the cross for the sins of the whole world.

## *Applications For Radical Economics*

To raise public awareness and make homeless people real to the public, invite homeless people to write their life stories, take photographs of their friends and living arrangements, and paint or draw scenes of street life, then have a public **"Homeless Art Exhibit"** at the city art gallery. Hold a press conference for promotion of the event. Return proceeds of sales to the homeless who contributed their art and to a repeat event or operation of a "Homeless Art Gallery." Get support from media, city government, and business associations.

Provide **free art classes** for homeless people who want to learn to draw and paint. Sell their art through the Homeless Art Gallery and downtown businesses where their art can be displayed.

Open a **coffee house** perhaps in conjunction with the homeless art gallery where homeless people can present their poetry, biographies, and other writing, as well as perform music. Use a cover charge to help with expenses and to compensate the homeless performers.

Set up a **"Free-Loan Bank"** in which your group lends money to the poor who are wanting to begin a business enterprise and who will pay you back when they succeed, with proceeds to be loaned again to another poor person. They should be required to meet with you for regular reports of their progress and to share ideas for success.

One day each week or each month, organize interested people in your church to go downtown to **distribute sandwiches** and inexpensive copies of the New Testament to homeless people. Distribute blankets, gloves, or head coverings in the winter.

Set up a permanent **downtown mission** outreach in the downtown area of your city where there is the most poverty. Do this in the name of your church such as "Downtown Christian Services."

Set up a **"Christian Counseling Service"** in the downtown area where people are suffering from homelessness and emotional problems.

The goal of **living simply** is worthwhile and needs an encouraging support group as suggested above. Here are a few ideas:

1. Make a conscious effort to minimize your wardrobe.
2. Eat third world food: beans and rice form a simple protein, then add a little cheese or chicken or fish and some vegetables.
3. Riding the bus and taking a taxi may be less costly than owning a car after you add up the expense of gas, insurance, parking, and repairs.
4. Share a single meal when two of you eat out.

The most radical application of Jesus' may involve **joining the poor**, becoming poor for the sake of the poor. Jesus became poor (II Cor.8:9), and Paul said, "Mind not high things, but condescend to men of low estate" (Rom.12:16). Make a move from your middle class or upper class community and live among the poorest and most troubled people in your city.

Set up a **Christmas Wish List** and **Birthday Wish List** website for homeless people you interview asking what they want. Put their stories on the site and notify the media to attract the public to give personalized gifts.

# Biblical References

## Part I: Radical Justice Economics

| MATTHEW | |
|---|---|
| 6:19 | 40,43,45 |
| 6:19,20 | 32 |
| 6:19-21 | 72 |
| 6:25 | 24 |
| 10:39 | 23 |
| 11:30 | 7 |
| 18:23-33 | 25 |
| 19:21 | 40,71 |
| 19:23 | 73 |
| 19:24 | 23 |
| 19:29 | 29,74 |
| 19:30 | 74 |
| 23:12 | 27 |
| 23:23 | 8 |
| 25 | 64 |
| 25:35-46 | 24 |
| 25:40 | 41 |

| MARK | |
|---|---|
| 9:35 | 27 |
| 10:13-16 | 29 |
| 12:41 | 41 |
| 12:41-44 | 72 |

| LUKE | |
|---|---|
| 1:51-54 | 37 |
| 1:53 | 18 |
| 3:4-14 | 38 |
| 3:8 | 18 |
| 3:10,11 | 18,23,24, 39,71 |
| 4:18 | 18,23,38, 76 |
| 6:20 | 20,23,39, 77 |
| 6:24 | 22,39,41, 46,47,73 |
| 6:30-35 | 58 |
| 6:34 | 63 |
| 6:34-35 | 61 |
| 7:21,22 | 39 |
| 7:22 | 18,77 |
| 9:23 | 7 |
| 11:5 | 59 |
| 11:41 | 40,72 |
| 12:21 | 41 |
| 12:33 | 20,32,40, 72 |
| 14:12-14 | 21 |
| 14:15-24 | 21 |
| 14:33 | 7,21,42, 71 |
| 16:8-12 | 41 |
| 16:9-12 | 42 |
| 16:13 | 42 |
| 16:13-15 | 75 |
| 16:15 | 42 |
| 16:19-25 | 41,46,73 |
| 18:1-8 | 64 |
| 18:22 | 19,32 |
| 19 | 64 |

| LUKE cont'd | |
|---|---|
| 19:8,9 | 19,32,40,72 |
| 19:20-23 | 65 |

| JOHN | |
|---|---|
| 12:8 | 32 |
| 12:42,43 | 77 |
| 19:38,39 | 77 |

| ACTS | |
|---|---|
| 2:44,45 | 43 |
| 4:32 | 77 |
| 4:32,34,35 | 43 |
| 4:32-5:11 | 43 |
| 4:34,35 | 25 |
| 20:30-35 | 66 |
| 20:34-35 | 45,78 |
| 20:35 | 28,46 |

| I CORINTHIANS | |
|---|---|
| 5:10,11 | 60 |
| 6:10 | 60 |

| II CORINTHIANS | |
|---|---|
| 8:1-4 | 77 |
| 8:2 | 44,78 |
| 8:9 | 44,78 |
| 8:12 | 44 |
| 8:14 | 26 |
| 8:14,15 | 44 |
| 8:15 | 26 |
| 9:6 | 24,41 |
| 9:7 | 44 |
| 9:8 | 26 |
| 9:8-11 | 45 |
| 9:10 | 26 |
| 9:11 | 26 |
| 9:13 | 46 |

| GALATIANS | |
|---|---|
| 6:10 | 45 |

| EPHESIANS | |
|---|---|
| 4:28 | 28,45 |
| 5:3 | 60 |

| COLOSSIANS | |
|---|---|
| 3:5-7 | 60 |

| I TIMOTHY | |
|---|---|
| 2:9-10 | 46 |
| 5:8 | 78 |
| 6:8 | 46,78 |
| 6:17-19 | 45,72 |
| 6:18 | 24 |
| 6:19 | 32 |

| II TIMOTHY | |
|---|---|
| 3:12 | 17 |

| I THESSALONIANS | |
|---|---|
| 3:12 | 46 |

| II THESSALONIANS | |
|---|---|
| 3:10 | 66 |

| HEBREWS | |
|---|---|
| 13:5 | 24,46 |

| JAMES | |
|---|---|
| 1:9,10 | 28 |

| JAMES cont'd | | I PETER | |
|---|---|---|---|
| 2:3,6 | 31 | 3:3 | 46 |
| 2:5 | 20,39 | | |
| 2:15,16 | 24 | REVELATION | |
| 2:24 | 76 | 3:17 | 17 |
| 5:1 | 39 | 3:17-18 | 46 |
| 5:4 | 67 | 18:3 | 47 |
| 5:5 | 22 | | |

## Part II: Radical Peace Politics

| MATTHEW | | 8:17 | 96 |
|---|---|---|---|
| 5:5 | 85 | 8:17,18 | 91 |
| 5:5,7,9 | 88 | 8:36 | 93 |
| 5:11,12 | 92 | | |
| 5:22 | 131 | I CORINTHIANS | |
| 5:25 | 131 | 4:12 | 94 |
| 5:39 | 85,90,131 | 6:1-6 | 131 |
| | | 6:7 | 106 |
| 11:12 | 87 | | |
| 16:24,25 | 86 | II CORINTHIANS | |
| | | 4:10,11 | 89 |
| JOHN | | 6:3-10 | 97 |
| 2:16 | 99 | 10:1 | 96 |
| 2:13-22 | 100 | 10:1-5 | 85 |
| 18:36 | 87 | 10:4,5 | 96 |
| | | 11:20 | 90,106,110 |
| ACTS | | | |
| 21:27-22:29 | 107 | | |
| 23:10-35 | 107 | GALATIANS | |
| 28:19 | 108 | 4:29 | 94 |
| | | | |
| ROMANS | | EPHESIANS | |
| 5:3,4 | 95 | 4:26 | 131 |
| 5:10 | 88 | 4:31 | 131 |

EPHESIANS cont'd
6:12         96-97
6:13-17      97

COLOSSIANS
3:13         131

I TIMOTHY
1:13         94
3:3          97

II TIMOTHY
2:9,12       96
2:24,25      110

II THESSALONIANS
1:5          91,95-96

TITUS
3:2          97

HEBREWS
10: 33,34    94
12:2-4       98
12:11        98

JAMES
1:19         130
5:6          90
5:10,11      92
12:19        131
12:20        98
12:21        97,98
13:1-7       102

I PETER
2:20         93,95,
             100
2:21         86
2:22,23      92
2:23         86
3:17,18      95
4:1          95
4:13         94

# Bibliography

## Primary Sources

Aristides (120 A.D.), *Apology.*

Athenagoras (177 A.D.), *A Plea for Christians.*

Clement of Alexandria (190 A.D.), *Instructor,* Vol. I and II.

Clement of Rome (96 A.D.), *Epistle to the Corinthians.*

*Epistle to Diognetus* (140 A.D.)

Hippolytus (220 A.D.), *Apostolic Tradition.*

Ignatius of Antioch (80-140 A.D.), *Epistle to the Ephesians.*

Irenaeus (180 A.D.), *Against Heresies,* Vol. IV.

Justin Martyr (150 A.D.), *Dialogue with Trypho.*

Origen (225 A.D.), *Against Celsus.*

*Preaching of Peter* (180 A.D.)

Shepherd of Hermas (135 A.D.), *Similitudes,* Vol. I.

Tertullian (200 A.D.), *On the Crown.*

## Secondary Sources

Batey, Richard. *Jesus and the Poor.* New York: Harper and Row, Publishers, 1972.

Campbell, Alexander in *Millennial Harbinger* June 1843.

Eager, George B. "Bank, Banking" in *The International Standard Bible Encyclopedia,* 1929 edition, Vol. I.

Ferguson, Everett. *Early Christians Speak.* Austin: Sweet Publishing, 1971.

Hoyt, R.S. *Europe in the Middle Ages.* New York: Harcourt, Brace and World, 1957.

Kittel, G., editor, *Theological Dictionary of the New Testament,* Vol. 2 and Vol.8.

Lovejoy, Arthur O. in *The Journal of the History of Ideas.* October, 1942.

Maloney, Robert P. "The Teaching of the Fathers on Usury" in *Vigilliae Christianae,* 27 [1973].

Nelson, Benjamin. *The Idea of Usury.* Chicago: University of Chicago Press, 1969.

Nicol,T., "Captivity" in *The International Standard Bible Encyclopedia,* 1929 ed., Vol.I.

Stone, Barton W. in *Christian Messenger*, June 1843.

Vine, W.E. "Lend, Loan" in *Expository Dictionary of New Testament Words*, 1966 edition.

Williams, Charles B. "Lend, Loan" in *International Standard Bible Encyclopedia*, 1929 edition, Vol.III.

# Index

abundance,
  22, 38, 77
  purpose of 26,
  44-45, 48
abundant giving,
  defined, 23-24,
  41, 42, 44
  result of, 25-
  26, 32-33, 72
Ambrose,
  luxury and
  hunger 48
Aristides, 48
assertiveness,
  in conflict,
  118, 121-122,
  124-125
Athenagoras,
  against legal
  action, 110
Augustine, 61, 108
  just war, 8, 114
Babylon,
  and the rich,
  47, 49
  Jews in, 55
Campbell, A., 53,
  lending and
  interest, 53-55
Celsus, pagan
  reference to
  pacifism, 112

cleansing,
  of temple, 101
Clement of
  Alexandria,
  on luxury,
  22, 30, 48
  on interest, 61
Clement of Rome,
  29, 48
conflict,
  biblical
  principles of,
  130-131
Constantine, 48,
  vision, 113
Cornelius,
  conversion, 99
court, 35, 104-106,
  108, 110, 131
Creath, Jacob,
  on interest, 66
daneizo,
  commercial
  loan, 58, 59, 64
Epistle To
  Diognetus, 48
eye of a needle, 22,
  73, 74
government,
  agents, 85, 99,
  102
  and Paul, 108
  court, 104-105

legislation, 85
   purpose of, 101-104
Hippolytus,
   forbidden roles, 111-112
Ignatius of Antioch,
   weapons, 109-110
interest, 51-67
   small, 55
   and usury, 56, 61, 62
Irenaeus,
   and war, 111
   and wealth, 30
Jerusalem church,
   and giving, 25, 44, 48, 77
Jesus ministry,
   poor and rich, 18-26, 38-39
   treasure, 32, 40
   radical, 7, 17, 33, 40
John the Baptist,
   proof of Messiah, 18, 77
   giving to poor, 18-19, 21, 77
   rich and poor, 37, 38, 71, 78
   non-violence, 180
judges, 37, 112, 113
judicial system, 103, 104, 106
just war doctrine, 8, 114
Justin Martyr,
   on war, 111
kichremi, personal loan, 58-59
Laodicea, 46, 49
liberality, 24, 26
   defined, 41, 72
loan, as a gift, 57, 59, 61, 65
   commercial, 54, 58, 63, 64
love,
   nature of, 26, 45, 88-89, 99, 109
luxury, 22, 30, 32, 42, 45, 46, 47, 48, 73, 75
Macedonians,
   giving, 25, 44, 46, 48
Mary,
   rich and poor, 18, 37, 38, 47, 48, 78
meekness, 85-91, 96-97, 99, 109, 114
Middle Ages,
   interest and profit, 56, 62,

needs,
	defined, 24, 78
Nippur, 55
non-resistance,
	57, 87-95, 99,
	105-106, 108-
	109, 110-112,
	113
Origen,
	on interest, 60,
	war, 111-112
patient endurance,
	85-88, 91-95,
	109
Paul,
	on court,
		105-106
	brought no
		charges,
		106-108
	on needs, 24, 78
	on giving,
		25-26, 28, 32,
		41, 44, 45, 72
	on government, 101-102
	on greed, 60, 65
	on love, 88
	persecution, 94
	on suffering,
		93, 94,
	on weapons,
		97, 98, 109
Peace, Prince of, 86

persecution,
	religious, 92, 94
	non-religious,
		92, 93
Pharisees,
	giving, 40, 72
Philippian jailer, 99
physical force, 99,
	100, 102, 103,
	104, 105, 107
plaintiff, 85, 104,
	105, 108, 110
pleonektes,
	unjust gain, 59,
	60
pleonexia,
	greed, 59, 60,
	64, 65,
poor,
	kingdom for,
		19, 20, 21, 23, 27
	gospel for, 18,
		23
power,
	giving up,
		124-125
pragmatism, 53, 63,
	67
Preaching of
	Peter, 29-30, 48
problem solving,
	117, 123,
	128-130
profit motive, 53,
	66-67

property,
   distributed,77
   God's, 42
   common,43
prophecy,
   peace in,86-87, 110-111
   non-resistance, 91-92,141
   poor in,18, 39,76-77
reflective listening, 117,126-127
Reformation,
   on interest, 62, 65
reversal,
   social order, 27-28
rich young ruler, 22-23,30,32,40, 45,71,72,75,78, 79
riches,
   trust in,32,75
secret disciples,
   rich men,77
Shepherd of Hermas,
   on riches,29,48
simple life,46,78
socialization,17,85
soldiers,85,98-99, 112-113

Stone, Barton W.,
   on interest, 63,66
suffering, joy of, 91, 93,94,109
swords,
   of apostles, 100-101
talents,
   parable of,64
Tertullian,
   on court, 110
   on force,113
   on interest,61
treasure in heaven, 19,20,22,32, 40-41,45,47, 71-72,74
unjust steward, 41-42
victim,
   church always, 87,91,93
voting,103-104
wealth,
   distribution, 19-20,27,32,40, 42,46-47
   purpose of,29, 41-42,44-45
weapons,
   Christian,85, 96-98,104,109
widow's mite, 23-24,41-42, 44,46,72

work ethic,28,45,
66,78
Zaccheus,19,21,
32,40,72,74

# *About the Author*

Daniel M. Keeran lives with his wife Jennie in Vancouver, British Columbia, Canada. Born in 1947, he is the youngest of four sons and the father of Phoebe and Seth. He has been a practicing psychotherapist since 1976.

He is a graduate of David Lipscomb University (BA, European History), the University of Kentucky (MA, Russian History), and Kent School of Social Work, University of Louisville (MSW, Clinical Social Work).

In 1985, he and his wife founded the Counsellor Training Institute that expanded to five cities in British Columbia and Nova Scotia.

He has also written *Healing Words: The Counsellor Training Course Manual*, *Therapeutic Journal: A Four-Month Diary for Counselling and Personal Growth*, *Soviet Policy Toward Evangelical Christians and Baptists from 1959 to 1970*, *Whites Living In The Black Community*, *If There Is No God: Meditations On Believing*, *Openings To God: Meditations for Spiritual Awareness*, *Reflections of the Cross*, *Gnostic Elements In Early Christianity*, *Mutual Understanding: Toward the Resolution of Social, Political, and Religious Issues*, *Homeless Partners: How To Help The Homeless*, and *Baptism and Baptisteries in the Ancient and Medieval World*.

He and his wife have founded a community awareness effort homelespartners.com, to connect people in the community to individual homeless people.

www.ingramcontent.com/pod-product-compliance
Lightning Source LLC
Chambersburg PA
CBHW050757160426
43192CB00010B/1554